THE HOLY GRAIL

THE HOLY GRAIL

CARTER SCOTT

© EDIMAT BOOKS Ltd. London
is an affiliate of Edimat Libros S.A.
C/ Primavera, 35 Pol. Ind. El Malvar
Arganda del Rey - 28500 (Madrid) Spain
E-mail: edimat@edimat.es

Title: *The Holy Grail*
Author: *Carter Scott*

ISBN: 84-9794-023-7
Legal Deposit: M-48223-2004

PRINTED IN SPAIN

INTRODUCTION

The great interest inspired by the Grail

The interest provoked by the Grail has several fundamental points. The first arises from literary related aspects, as represented by popular, cult and spiritual literature, within an esoteric and above all religious framework. Old traditions, many of them Celtic, were the starting point for these legends, which were skilfully constructed into poems and novels rooted in the spirit of knights and cavaliers of the time, and which needed the power of literature to become myths, and a vocation for the sons of nobles and the haute bourgeoisie.

Another interesting and perhaps the most effective factor, was the clever application of the element of mystery. Although the Greeks and Celts had already used this narrative style, the writers of the Grail, most of whom were troubadours and familiar with aristocratic tastes, created the adventure novel, or in essence, the universal novel. In Homer's The Odyssey, Ulysses is travelling towards his native lands, where his beautiful wife, Penelope, and son, Telemachus, await his return. Ulysses, though, is forced to undertake a search making him stop at several islands, each more dangerous than the last. In the tales of the Grail, it is the pursuit of something sublime: the conquest of a bowl which is of divine origin, and thus comparable to God.

The legends of the knights

In order to attempt an analysis of the enigma of the Grail, we must consider the legends of chivalry while ignoring the superficial aspect. This calls for an investigation of the myths, epic poems and the epics told throughout history. When specialists become too analytical, they look into the subconscious of the creators of these myths. In certain cases, this is a valid technique, but it would appear excessive when it comes to evaluating poems and novels written during a particular era, under certain conditions, and which, above all, were sentimentalised for entertainment.

It is true to say that very few, if any, of the creators of these tales enjoyed total freedom in their writing. They depended on a patron, who was usually a prince or a nobleman, the lords of the feudalist world, where democracy was unheard of. Literary writing has always taken time, during which they needed to eat, sleep, keep the fire stoked and protect themselves against illness, needs that were increased when the writer had a family to support. Authors therefore needed a patron, who was paid back through control over what the author wrote, often under the condition of a mention on the first page of the work.

Another very important point is that these works were not sold, because if they were considered of interest they were handed over to the copyists or scribes, who had the task of writing copies that were to be given as gifts. Of course there was also another, more effective, form of distribution, which was by means of the troubadours, who discovered the tales and took care to spread them around on their travels. The more honourable among them quoted the author, and those that were not adopted the tales as their own, resulting in various personal adaptations.

'Shroud the interesting parts in mystery'

There is a literary motto which goes *Shroud the interesting parts in mystery, and make the significant parts clear*. Emperor Julianus made a similar remark: *What appears to be credible in a myth is precisely what shows us the path to the truth. Therefore, the more paradoxical and extraordinary the enigma, the more it seems to warn us not to trust the naked word, so that we suffer at the hands of the hidden truth. Only in this way will we find what is truly interesting.*

The point appears to be as simple as the tale of the doors, in which the main character of the story is told that he may open all the doors apart from one particular one, by which the prohibited door becomes the only door, because the character can think of nothing else but what may be hidden behind it. It is possible that use of such tactics is unintentional, but the careful reader is given to assume that the author of the story had studied the human mind in depth, and knew very well how to stimulate it.

While his companions sleep, the knight remains alert as the spell could come from an apparently innocuous fountain.

This strategy is adopted to great success by the writers on the subject of the Grail: in their tales they play to the desire to conquer a superior objective through a search which only those who have consciously prepared themselves for can take on. The characters therefore become heroes, though at no point do they stop being normal men who are ravaged by doubt in the face of danger. They then overcome that doubt and danger, in an exceptional show of bravery. The danger may come from an apparently simple source, which then releases a curse. The knight must then act as quickly as possible, with nothing to help him but his own wits.

A very unsatisfied society

At this point it is necessary to examine society at the end of the twelfth century. In those times life went on at horse speed, or in other words, the processes of social evolution either took centuries to develop, or happened very suddenly as a result of invasions such as those of the barbarians. However, the normal thing was for changes to take a long time to come into effect.

European society had emerged from the tenth century in a state of exhaustion, tormented by prophets predicting apocalypses and the end of the world. Most roadways were filled with processions of penitents, flogging themselves to redeem themselves of their sins.

When they became aware of the falseness of this belief, they should have all returned to the lands that they had abandoned. However, they noticed that nearby another danger was lurking: the force of Islam, which had conquered almost all of the Iberian Peninsula, claimed the Holy Land, and already controlled more than half the Mediterranean as well as all of North Africa and part of South-east Europe.

The Roman Church organised a Crusade, which managed to recapture Jerusalem, but it was then lost again in the twelfth century. The enemy had become a great threat, so much so that Christianity, together with the Pope, financed new Crusades. At the same time, orders of monk-warriors were formed, such as the Order of the Templar. They formed a whole range of forces, which were permanently lacking in a sense of unity, perhaps because they needed to believe deeply in what they were fighting for, and above all in the responsibility that they were taking on.

This is why the appearance of poems and novels about the Holy Grail sated the thirst for myth, by offering one with which Europe could identify. The spirit of the lands was ready to take a radical step, at a time when the tide of change was strong.

Finding paradise

Two cultures were feuding in the Near East. Swords of European princes and Oriental caliphs crossed. While they were busy killing each other or saving their skins, they were gradually gaining an insight into each other's culture and it was leaving an impression. For instance, the ferocious warriors took an enemy fortress in defence of the cross. While capitalizing on the defence it afforded they realized there were fountains with different types of water, well-kept gardens, harems and other signs of sensuality that they ended up envying. The ones they had called 'Saracen dogs' washed at least once a day while they themselves went for weeks without doing so. They used scent whereas the Christians smelt as if they lived in pigsties. Above all, they knew how to surround themselves with the most inviting pleasures.

Malcolm Godwin in his work "The Holy Grail: Its Origins, Secrets and Meaning Revealed" enlightens us on this point:

The exotic atmosphere of the desert and the descriptions of the rich and civilised paradises in the Holy Land seduced the whole of Europe, while the quest for the most sacred city, in 1099, caused an upsurge in religious fervour in both princes and peasants. But it was also a time when political power in Europe was fragmented and armed groups were subjugating farmers and reducing their land to moors. In the last decade, even the elements worked against the poor, ruining harvests that led to famine with devastating consequences and terrible disease. To support the Crusade, many landowners pledged their properties to the Church as security, with land subsequently becoming drastically devalued. Farmers traded in their impoverished lands for the promise of eastern delights, both spiritual and carnal. The Church was not only generously dispensing indulgences, but it also encouraged people to partake in the expedition against the infidels by declaring automatic expiation for their sins.

Although some crusaders could have been opportunists, their sincerity and religious fervour were undeniable, as was the compassion of many knights and pilgrims. And the clergy of Rome, well aware of every single advantage the situation presented, encouraged a true spiritual quest. The market-place was flooded with supernatural and miraculous sacred relics.

Every abbot and ecclesiastical institution promoted their own particular saint together with his sacred remains, the total number of pilgrims received and the frequency or success of his miracles. The Grail legend was born out of this religiously overcharged and hysterical climate. But while everybody was looking to the Holy Places in greed, a balancing factor was arising from Merlin's Island in the remote North-East.

Where should we site the Grail?

Malcolm Godwin claims that Merlin's Island was the home to the Grail, so we will have to go to North-East England, as the heroes are King Arthur, the Round Table and all his knights. Other scholars, however, suggest different places such as the Pyrenees, Spain and the Holy Land as they believe that the authors of the Grail legend used symbolic names, the purpose being to conceal the real ones. We will expand on this point later.

The famous expert on myths Joseph Campbell tells us the following in one of his books:

One of the main errors of many of those who have interpreted the symbols is to read them as references to scenes, earthly or beyond, and historical events, real or imaginary, not as mysteries relating to the human spirit: for example, they promised land, like Canaan; they spoke of celestial paradise as part of the sky, they reported the Israelites crossing the Red Sea in the same way as a journalist would. But, in actual fact, one of the glorious elements (of the Grail tradi-

tion) is that in dealing with religious topics, they translate them from the realm of imagined facts to a clearly mythological language; in this way they are not perceived as being conditioned by time rather they are timeless; they do not speak to us of miracles that happened a long time ago but of potential miracles that could happen inside of us, here now and forever.

This is the nature of the myth that deserves to be immortalized: its present day application. We can respect scholars' rights to look for its origins because that is what we are going to do; however, we should not overlook the fact that as soon as a literary work enters the sphere of public awareness it ceases to belong to him, in part, and it begins to belong to everyone.

In one way the myth of the Grail legend is similar to Arthur Conan Doyle's experience when he created the superb character of Sherlock Holmes: he found himself with a mythical character that had outstripped him, as his character had become more famous than he himself. When he 'killed' Sherlock Holmes in one of his novels, tired of his destiny, he had to bring him back to life by public demand. As soon as a fictional creation acquires such strength, it is appropriated and no questions are asked as to who their creators are. This is a very unfair situation as 'all children have parents' but the custom is already established. Besides, deep down, all authors love to create myths, because through them, they live on.

The importance of women

We know that the Celts considered men and women as equals in all senses, even regarding weaponry. Yet they did not lead military manoeuvres for survival purposes, as they had to take care of the home and children. The concept is not a sexist one if we consider that the average age of death was twenty-four and that one out of every three babies born into the world died. After all, somebody had to keep the dwelling fit for living, take care of the home and tend the animals, apart from the elderly and children.

In the Grail legend women appeared in many facets: as the lover, heroine, spiritual guide or witch.

Yet in the twelfth century, women were perceived in a very negative light indeed, not surprisingly, they were treated worse than beasts in many places. Authors such as Bernard of Cluny spread this notion. He wanted to justify the population rise through his poem "Scorn for the World", in which he portrayed women as the cause of all indecency. He accused them of the most execrable offences on account of possessing an innate talent for disguising their malice; they were incapable of living decently, they fornicated with all men and never stopped having babies, who then became victims of their mothers' corruption...Could anybody have ever believed such a load of nonsense?

In those times, the few women that could read did not find these remarks flattering, while the others had their work cut out bringing up children, waiting for their husbands who were always at war or working the land, in the house and wherever needed. Most women were slaves to a system that had been conceived to undermine them, using them as 'animals of work or pleasure'.

The inferior sex

Saint Thomas of Aquinas was considered to be one of the highest representatives of scholastic philosophy. He taught in Europe's main universities. This did not prevent him from having a very unfavourable opinion of women as he showed in his work "Summa Theologica":

That is why, to quote Genesis, 1.27, he created him in the image of God *he adds,* he created them male and female. *He says 'them' in the plural, and Saint Agustin affirmed,* so that it is not understood that one of the two sexes had been together in the same individual.

But the image of God is found in man in a secondary sense, and is not to be found in woman.

Man is therefore the beginning and end of woman, the same as God is the beginning and the end of all creation. That is why the apostle says that man is the image and glory of God, and woman is the glory of man *and to show why he says this he adds* man has not been created because of woman, but the woman because of man.

Discrimination is clearly evident. In line with this reasoning, women are completely dominated by men, just as in the ancient world, maybe even more harshly.

The emancipation the troubadours offered

The troubadours did not consider carnal love to be a sin, not even setting one's sights at a married woman, so that the adoration of women was taken to the loftiest heights. The Countess of Die exclaimed vehemently:

All ladies, even virgins, can love, if they find a man who is right for them.

Choosing a man became a novelty for these women, who unashamedly took advantage of the fact. They had previously

13

had to wait to be courted, always demonstrating their honesty, but as soon as the troubadours adopted this idea, they turned into enticers of desire. When they were attracted to a young man, they did not try to signal their interest to him in a round about way, if required, they seduced him with all sorts of talents, without turning their noses up at magic charms.

We should bear in mind that these 'story singers' populated the regions of Toulouse and Languedoc, and for the most part, the stories were gallant, so presumably, sensuality was in the air. Other ladies' love affairs, made into verse, invited those listening to them to become the leading lady, even though they were not terribly passionate or dramatic. And the same occurred with the relationship between Queen Guinevere, King Author's wife, and Lancelot of the Lake in the Grail legend, which can be considered to be pure provocation.

The three that managed to succeed

Only three knights had the iron will to succeed in the quest for the Holy Grail and then to contemplate it without suffering any ill fate. The fortunate men were Galahad, who was seen as the 'irreproachable, virgin hero', Perceval, the naïve one with a vocation to be a saint, and Bors, who seemed the most ordinary and humble of all the members of the Round Table. He was the only one to take the news of his success to Camelot.

As far as Perceval is concerned, after suffering his first failure on account of his dopiness and ignorance, he had a second chance. But before this, he had to go through a kind of atonement that lasted five years until he found the perfect path to take him to the castle of the Injured King or 'Fisher King' who was the custodian of the Waste Land. The hero healed the king, and in turn, prosperity was restored throughout the kingdom, but he died; he was an old man and it had been his wish for a long time.

The Church remained silent

From the first poem to the last novel written on the Holy Grail during the Middle Ages, historians believe that one hundred and fifty years elapsed, a relatively short time for that period. Authors used countless symbols, all taken from ancient cultures, but presented in the most suggestive of ways.

As the Grail was also tied to Catharism, a Christian heresy, the Church did not dare acknowledge it openly. Few priests made reference to it in their writings and it is not known if bishops, cardinals or the Pope did. They are believed to have feared that open support for a legend that was excessively charged with pagan and esoteric elements could have given rise to a schism. However, they passively allowed the Grail to get confused with the chalice of the Last Supper. Furthermore, they did not ban Robert de Boron's book *Joseph of Arimathea*, which directly introduced Christianity into the Grail storyline, and they almost applauded the appearance of *Perceval* by Wolfram von Eschenbach, on account of his work being the most Christian of all.

It is the quest that counts

The Grail Legend should be seen as a universal adventure: the quest for the best in each person. The heroes that started this journey doubted their readiness and went in quest of the impossible. They carried on because what counted was not giving in to the weaknesses of the flesh, the obstacles that would arise and the enemies, even supernatural ones that obstructed their way. The spirit had to be kept alive.

These privileged individuals could love, suffer and make mistakes because they were modelled on humans, never on gods; male readers will identify with their constant battle more than female readers on account of being more intrigued and excited by adventures. The fascination of the Grail enigma was total as it rested on the idea of the goal to be achieved. This innate driving force has been present in all of us right from the beginning.

Yet it is worth asking ourselves these questions: Why do we need to search for the impossible? To what extent is the Holy Grail a useful outlet for our passions? Is it true the Church manipulated this legend while appearing uninterested? How many authors were there? How many symbols are used in the writings that should have been regarded as 'straightforward chivalrous stories'?

Our aim is to answer these questions along with others while offering an enjoyable read capable of fuelling the reader's desire to continue investigating the subject.

Chapter I
THE ORIGINS OF THE MYTH

The sacred cup

It has been suggested that the symbol of the sacred cup is linked to the most primitive cultures, given that it appears in cave paintings. It cannot be any old cup, which filled with wine, inebriates and introduces an uncontrolled element into a situation. It was believed to work miracles, both its content and the object itself on account of its shape and the material it was made out of, and that this power could be passed on to the bearer.

Primitive man was completely ignorant of all this, yet he was aware of his hostile environment where he could fall victim to vicious animals, diseases and Nature, when he was not under threat from other tribes. He was beginning to recognise poisonous plants and to hunt. Priests kept the fire alive and started to fill caves with sacred objects and fetishes. This explains why their dead were buried in peculiar tombs shaped like a reclining woman with 'a cup and a ring' engraved on them to ensure eternal peace.

In many countries, legends referred to the sky as an inverted bowl that the gods used to cover the Earth while the great heavenly bodies, the Sun and the Moon, were filled with divine liquors. These liquors could only be served to the heroes in gold cups which gave them superhuman strength

17

and virtual immortality, allowing them to rival the gods. The Vedic god Indra robbed the Sun of its fire and the Moon of its divine drink (soma), which it used to transform its spear into a fertility instrument: by simply stabbing it into barren land the area was rendered fertile providing two or three crops a year.

In the Holy Grail legends, the spear has a special meaning. Indra's feat of freeing water is on a par with Perceval's; when he healed the 'Fisher King' he caused the rivers to flow, the springs and the wells filled with the same intensity as in *those years when no curse weighed them down.*

The Greeks' idea of the cup

In Greek philosophy, the cup was envisaged as being shaped like a crater or goblet, and was used to represent the womb of creation, the celestial vessel in which the basic elements of existence were combined. This mixture was given to newly born souls to bestow them with intelligence, which would then lead to constructive wisdom. Plato wrote about Vulcan's crater in which the gods mixed the Sun's light; and in his "Psychogony" he mentions another two vessels, the scent for universal nature was made in one, while in the other *the minds of human beings.* Later, Plato wrote that when drinking from the crater *the soul was dragged to a new body, intoxicated and wishing to have another mouthful, and this way it became heavier and returned to Earth.*

G.R.S. Mead, in his study of the Orphean mysteries, linked these vessels to the cup of Dionysius from which spouted inspiration, and affirmed that Orpheus *placed many others similar around the Solar Table,* that according to Orphean cosmology was the centre and beginning of the universe. To Mead this meant each of the spheres was, simultaneously, a cup that contained a scent, that of creation. Here we have a cup conceived as a cosmic vessel and a table that foreshadows the Round Table, upon which the Holy Grail was later to appear, as a symbol of divine power.

The Celts gave birth to the mystery

The large number of legends linked to the Holy Grail do not agree on a description for the vessel, nor with the powers it possessed, which prompted Roger S. Loomis to write: *The authors of texts on the Grail seem to enjoy contradicting each other on the most important points.*

Yet the Grail can be found in pagan mythologies long before Christendom claimed it as theirs. A large number of Celtic myths took place within an unreal universe of absolutely impossible dreams, but were clearly formulated by the Druids (the magic priests of the Celts) with so much literary force that they enthralled listeners.

In the festivities that Hyperborean warriors held, before beer and mead set their heads spinning, one of the main entertainments was listening to stories. In them, many objects were referred to like the famous serving dish of Rhydderch 'the Generous' on which any type of food appeared that its owner wished for. However, there was no vessel as prodigious as the magic cauldron. The god Goibniu used it to make a beer that gave eternal life to whoever drank it. Dagda, the father of gods in Irish Celtic legend, was said to have a saucepan that was only used to cook food for heroes because through it they received ever-lasting life.

The magic cauldron and other wonders

Celtic legends are divided into different cycles according to the countries or regions they originated from. The 'Branches of the Mabinogis' belong to Welsh legend. They are about the Mac Llyr family who, on account of their divine character, are considered to be 'Children of the sea', therefore similar to the Irish god Lir.

The basic characters are Branwen and her brother Bendigeidfran, who is also known as Bran 'the Blessed'. The story started with the wedding of Branwen and Matholwch, the king of Ireland. As Efnisien, another of Branwen's brothers, did not accept the union he insulted Matholwch wherever he went. The more he shouted the more furious he became and ended up mutilating his brother-in-law's horses when they were being put into the stables at Harlech.

They managed to calm Matholwch down only after he had demanded adequate compensation comprising several valuable objects and above all the magic cauldron, or bloody revenge. It had been forged in Ireland and its main quality was that it could bring dead heroes back to life by simply boiling them inside.

However, the marriage had been seriously harmed, as could be seen when Matholwch and Branwen arrived in Ireland by boat. The husband treated the wife like a slave going to the extreme of locking her in the castle kitchen where the person in charge was under orders to beat her and make her do the worst tasks. However, all this was kept secret to create the illusion that the couple got along very well.

The long-suffering queen eventually found a way of saving herself although it took her a long time to achieve, because she had to train a starling for the purpose in secret. Thanks to this bird Bendigeidfran found out about the humiliating situation that his sister was being subjected to. This led him to mobilize his entire army and then to declare war on Ireland.

Cauldron of Gundestrop, made of silver gilt and conserved in Denmark. It could be the Celtic magic receptacle in which the corpses of heroes were 'boiled' to bring them back to life.

The legend describes Bendigeidfran as a gigantic being, so big that he could not fit into an ordinary house. He was capable of walking on the waves of the sea without ever sinking regardless of how far he went. While he was fighting a battle, Bendigeidfran was fatally wounded by a poisoned spear. Unfortunately he could not be 'boiled' in the magic cauldron because it was in the king of Ireland's possession. As the infection spread, the gigantic hero asked his friends to cut off his head. They did it without causing him any pain. It was the only way he could stay alive, as he had not lost his immortality.

Lastly, Bendigeidfran's head ordered them to take it to White Mount in London where it was to be buried facing eastwards so as to prevent foreign armies from invading the island of Britain. However, the road was so long that it took twenty years. During this time, the head talked to the men. It was also used as a talisman to protect against countless dangers. This was how they arrived at Harlech where they settled and afterwards they moved to the Happy Beyond of Wales, a place that was cheered by the singing of three magic birds from Rhiannon. It was where Branwen died of sorrow, the sister of the gigantic hero who was nothing more than a head. Her sorrow is symbolic of the fact that no peace agreement was signed between Wales and Ireland.

The most important details of this legend have to be seen, seeking a parallel with the Grail, in the magic cauldron, which is able to bring heroes back to life. The same applies to that talking head, which offers advice and goes on conserving immortality without the need to receive food or water.

Greek roots

An object similar to the magic cauldron can be found in Greek mythology. Plato describes two vessels in his "Psychogony" that were used by the divine creator of the universe. One of them was used to *mix all the souls of Universal Nature while in the other the creator carefully modelled the intelligence of human beings.*

Meanwhile, in the work "Corpus Hermeticum" which is attributed to the Greek prophet Hermes Trimegistus, a sacred cup is mentioned, which is also referred to as a crater inside which the gods boiled the elements of life. Each soul obtained its portion of intelligence and wisdom through the cosmic substance.

We have only shown a small sample of mythical components to which many more should be added. They gradually configured the essence of an object capable of granting eternal life. It was worthy of becoming the fanciful goal of the best, of noble men initiated in the art of weaponry. This is how the foundations of the Holy Grail were laid.

Chapter II
THE POEM OF CHRÉTIEN DE TROYES

The knights needed it

The Middle Ages are associated with knights, but they would have been nothing without myths, one in particular tied them to religion. This myth had to have a certain quality that put it out of reach, but that could be presented in a sublime light to make it seem real. As they did not want to sever their ties with the Roman Church, they searched in their origins until they found the ideal myth, namely, the Holy Grail or the chalice of the Last Supper that Jesus Christ shared with his apostles.

However, this objective was attained by way of a French romance written by Chrétien de Troyes, one of the most famous authors of the period. He was responsible for several works of far-reaching success, but it was not until his mature years that he decided to create what was to be his most prestigious work: *Le roman de Perceval* or *Le conte du Graal*. He was thought to have written it in 1188, the same year as the fall of Jerusalem, therefore the West, full of fear, was forced to look towards the Holy Land.

While word of the Crusade was spreading to every corner of Europe, being thundered from pulpits, a simple book was put into circulation. Even though few could read, copyists began receiving commissions that meant they had to multiply their efforts to cover the great demand for copies. But it is worth pointing out that printing was not to be invented for another three centuries, in those days the task was done manually. There was another vehicle that was far more efficient, namely, word of mouth. Celtic bards essentially used this medium as they were banned from writing. They were the times of troubadours and minstrels, the ones who could spread stories at the speed of a horse. They were very much in demand in castles and abbeys where the fascinating *Le conte du Graal* was starting to achieve fame. It could be said that it reached the ears of the most important people at the right time.

Meanwhile, Chrétien de Troyes was still in the Count of Champagne's court. Curiously, he did not dedicate his most famous creation to them but instead to Philippe of Alsace, a Flemish count on whose lips he first heard the story according to the first page. However, this is thought not to be true, rather, it should be considered as being a literary tool used to flatter a nobleman. This was quite commonplace as it was customary to seek out financial support in this way or at least political backing for each literary work; in such a way it would gain acceptance more readily and not produce a confrontation with the judges.

Nobody until then had written about the Grail, but the legend was known albeit in many different forms. It loomed like a faint, almost imperceptible power. The word Grail had also been used in some other writings and pronounced by different religious orders. Yet nobody had thought of this myth until Chrétien de Troyes' work became known.

The son of the 'Widowed Lady'

In "Le conte du Graal", the child who had the great honour bestowed upon him did not know his real name. He was the son of the 'Widowed Lady', who had lost two sons to war, while her husband had lost the use of his legs and suffered a very painful existence until his death. That is why the child was breastfed for over two years until he began teething. Later, he was to be educated far away from the world, always with his protectress, so that he should not know violence in any of its forms. Yet he was to learn to hunt using simple darts.

One day when he was in the woods, he heard the sound of horses' hooves and other sounds unfamiliar to him. He did not hide because he did not know what fear was. He saw two knights in suits of armour go by and he thought they were devils. As he was so shocked, the strange figure stopped to tell him that they were knights of King Arthur. The boy watched them recede into the distance in silence, while deep down he had the sensation that he had seen angels. From that moment on he never stopped asking his mother to let him go to the court of King Arthur.

The 'Widowed Lady's young son arriving at King Arthur's castle, which would be the mythical Camelot.

After a few years the separation came; but beforehand, the 'Widowed Lady' took care to advise her son to be cautious and not to ask strangers questions or talk to them either. When it was time for her son to leave, she stayed on the other side of the bridge and the young rider crossed it practically without looking back. And he was so determined to leave at all costs that he did

25

not even go back when he saw that his mother had fallen to the ground in a faint.

In King Arthur's court

Apparently, this youth was so naïve as to think that merely wishing for something entitled him to have it. That is why he ended up taking a ring off a young lady, stealing her meat pie and lastly giving her a playful kiss. As he also did not know shame, he went to King Arthur's court and entered the main room on horseback. He did not take the trouble to ask for permission as he was not aware of that obligation. Yet nobody reproached him as it happened at the most awkward moment; Arthur was being slapped by a knight who had previously added a potion to the cup he had snatched away from Queen Guinevere. Furthermore, he made so bold as to challenge all the members of the Round Table.

While Guinevere retired to her chambers, where she was not only in intense pain but also outraged, the young son of the 'Widowed Lady' audaciously killed the rebel knight with his lancet, and afterwards returned the queen's cup to her. As the seneschal Kay believed it to be a stroke of luck that he had taken the life of one of the most feared men in the kingdom, he unabashedly made fun of the stranger's rash behaviour, and the boy promised to take his revenge for those words. A little later he left the castle taking with him his victim's armour, without waiting to be armed as a knight by King Arthur.

The young man rode through the woods feeling very uncomfortable in his armour, as he did not know how to wear it, and at the same time he found it difficult to guide his horse. Luckily for him he reached the castle of Gornemant of Goort, who was to become his master and teach him about weaponry and everything else a knight had to know, such as nobility, the duty to protect the weakest, and not to talk more than necessary.

The passionate meeting with Blanchefleur

Months later, the hardened young lad, already an excellent horse-rider, in his continuous wandering arrived at another castle, where he was received by the very beautiful Blanchefleur. But in the beginning she thought he was dumb, as she did not know that the stranger had confined himself to listening, following the advice his mother and Gornemant had given him. When he did speak, it was merely to disclose that he was an aspiring knight.

That same night, the lady visited him in his chambers to talk to him about the enemies whose intention it was to drive her from her lands. Finally, they shared the same bed and the young man discovered all the great secrets of love...*The maiden suffered his kisses, although I do not think that she found them so terrible. That is how they rested that night, mouth to mouth, until the morning that brought the new day.*

The next day, the young son of the 'Widowed Lady' showed that the new-found passion had not drained his strength, or astuteness as he vanquished his love's enemies: Clamadeu and his seneschal Anguingueron. Once he had disarmed and brought them to the ground, he ordered them to go to King Arthur's court, where they were to be taken prisoner. At the same time, they had to take a message of vengeance to Kay.

A few weeks of love went by, until the young man felt guilty for having abandoned his mother on the other side of the bridge without helping her when he had seen her faint. He set out, but did not know what direction to head in. That is why he became a vagabond, and did not cease to fight off knights. Once he had defeated them he sent them to King Arthur's castle.

The young man did not realise that having been mollycoddled for such a long time by his mother had made him invincible. In fact, he fought whenever he was challenged because he knew no fear. The wish to fight never came from him. He never forgot this rule because, if he became the challenger, his triumph would be devoid of all nobility.

Faced with the mysterious Fisher King

The young aspiring knight had barely reached puberty when he found a spot called *Terre Gaste* where all was barren on account of a magic curse. The trees looked withered, and only weeds grew from the ground that not even the hungriest of animals would eat. A large number of women were forced to live there like weak Amazons, as their parents, brothers or other relatives were dead.

The Fisher King was on the other side of the river. His advice was linked to the Grail castle.

But in that place there also lived the Fisher King, a cripple whose only pleasure was to be had in the river that surprisingly ran deep enough for boats to sail in. And from one of them he greeted the young man as soon as he saw him reach one of the banks. He immediately pointed out the way to the Grail castle to him using the best words from his repertory and without further ado he persuaded him to go there.

The young hero entered the great building where, once again, he found himself in the presence of the Fisher King, who was resting on a special divan for big banquets. He invited him sit down on the other divan and then he gave him a sword to him that only he would be able to wield, but that would break if used to do wrong.

While they were quietly talking, a groom came out of a room holding a dazzling white lance at its mid-point. He walked in front of the hearth and the couches where they were talking. Both of them could see a drop of blood welling up at the tip of the lance which soon began running down until it reached the groom's hand. At that moment another couple of smartly dressed servants appeared carrying gold jewel-inlaid lamps. Some ten candles were burning in each of the lamps. A grail appeared in the hands of the beautiful and kind damsel dressed in finery walking behind the servants.

As soon as she entered with the Grail, the light shone so bright that the candles became faint, as happens to the moon and stars when the sun comes out. Another damsel appeared behind the first one carrying a silver chopping block. The Grail that preceded it had been worked with the purest gold and set with the most precious stones; they must have been chosen from among the most valuable and varied to have ever been extracted from the ground and sea; but none of them could be compared to those set in the gleaming Grail. Just as the lance passed before Perceval and the Fisher King, so did the damsels until they finally disappeared in another room...

One damsel was holding the Grail while the other was carrying a silver chopping block.

Moments before, the young son of the 'Widowed Lady' had had to hold on tightly to the table so as not to fall to the floor, so dumbfounded was he by the scene, and at the same time he had had to cover his eyes with his hands. And when he managed to take them away, he had great difficulty in getting used to the light until he was able to look at the Grail carried by the beautiful angelic damsel. This was the prelude to a magnificent banquet at which the finest dishes were served. The young man had never seen anything like it. He ate heartily on being invited to do so to discover that everything tasted exquisitely. While they were feasting the Grail was there in the middle of the large room, shining brighter than ten suns and too dazzling even to look at.

What had happened?

Once the Grail had disappeared, with so much food and drink before him, his curiosity seemed to have escaped from his head and gone down to his stomach. A strange drowsiness started to come over him and at the same time the memory of his mother removed any remaining desire to speak… Everything that was happening to him at the Grail castle turned out to be rather strange.

Finally he fell asleep and on waking up he discovered, to his bemusement, that he was in a completely empty room. Still bewildered, he managed to stand up to leave the castle. Nobody appeared to help him. A little later he thought that what had happened was punishment for having left his mother to die on the other side of the bridge.

Suddenly, he realized that the drawbridge of Grail castle was closing behind him, which made him think that he could never enter it again. He decided to take to the road after finding his horse and armour. He was also carrying the sword that the Fisher King had given to him.

Perceval the Welshman

A few hours later, the aspiring knight found himself in a clearing in the woods before a young girl who was on her knees crying beside a beheaded body. He dismounted his horse and when he was about to help the distressed girl she turned away and…her face filled with astonishment!

You must be my cousin Perceval the Welshman, she whispered almost unable to support herself.

I do not understand, Madame, said the aspiring knight taken aback. *I have always been called the boy, the young man, or the son of the 'Widowed Lady'…*

You were taught to ask no questions, the young girl went on. *That is why when you were inside the Castle you forgot to ask the vital question "what is the Grail?" If you had, at this moment the Fisher King would have been healed and all this land would have been prosperous once again. You will have to be on your guard about something else too, make sure that the sword you are carrying does not break while you are fighting! However, if it does happen you can go to 'lake below Cotoatre' where the 'blacksmith Trebuchet' lives. Never forget that he forged it and only his hands and furnace can repair it!*

The young man silently listened as a range of emotions washed over him. On one hand he liked the idea that he could count on that name and on the other, the reason for his failure weighed almost fatally on his heart, leaving him breathless for a few minutes. However, on hearing the part about the sword he realized that there was still a future for him.

He took leave of his cousin after helping her to bury the beheaded corpse of her friend. He then continued his aimless journey until he found himself before the young girl whose ring, meat pie and kiss he had stolen. The loss of her ring had made her very unhappy and Perceval was sure to put it right. Later, he continued his route and it took him to the surroundings of Camelot where King Arthur's impressive castle was to be found.

A few drops of blood in the snow

It had been snowing and the ground appeared to be covered in a thick blanket of whiteness. In the meadow, Perceval was contemplating he caught sight of a goose that had been wounded by a falcon and three drops had fallen on the snow. The son of the 'Widowed Lady' dismounted and went over to the red stains and *the bright colours reminded him of his friend*

Blanchefleur. The memories were so pleasant that he forgot where he was. The colour in her cheeks stood out against the white of her face just like the three drops of blood on the white blanket that covered the ground...

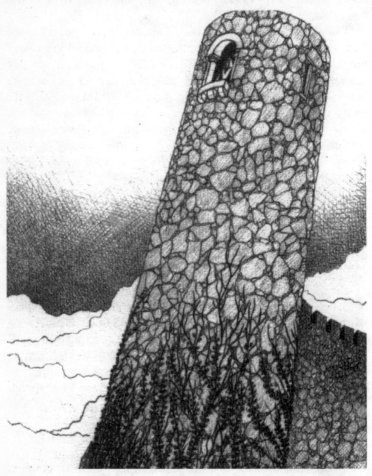

To save the young prisoner from the castle of Montesclaire the knights defending the Proud Castle had to be defeated.

Perceval entered into such a deep trance that he stayed there for several days. This reached King Arthur's ears and he ordered some of his best knights to go and persuade him to stop sending him prisoners. But Perceval had decided to remain like a statue while his brain evoked thoughts about his love. That is why he only pushed those that reached him. Obviously having Kay near, he pushed harder. Finally, it was Gawain that managed to convince him to leave the place; he was not the best public speaker in Camelot for nothing. He was also a loyal friend who was said to be capable of giving his life for another if justified.

Perceval was appointed a knight and for some months he underwent initiation tests and trials as well as other activities that made him fall into his bed at night completely exhausted.

The extremely ugly damsel on a mule

One day, a damsel mounted on a mule. She could not go unnoticed...*You never did see such greyish metal for a neck, and no less for her hands. Her eyes were simple cavities, no bigger than those of a rat; her nose resembled a cat's and a monkey's and her lips those of a donkey and an ox, teeth yellow like egg-yolk and a billy-goat beard, a hump in the middle of her chest, her back looked twisted, her kidneys and shoulders looked just fine to lead a dance, a hump on her back and twisted legs, like wicker poles, impressive for dancing.*

The damsel started to insult Perceval in front of everyone, on account of not having asked the question in the Grail castle. She reminded him that because of his mistake, wives ended up losing their husbands, hundreds of horses perished and everything was devastated forever in those lands. However, when she had calmed down, she spoke of a different objective, saving the young prisoner from the castle of Montesclaire, and to do so the knights that defended the Proud Castle had to be overpowered.

All the members of the Round Table volunteered to carry out this mission but Gawain was the one who headed out in that direction. In the meantime, Perceval decided to dismount in search of the Castle where he had failed on account of not having asked at the time. There he was going to find out *who used the Grail and to find the bleeding spear.*

33

Unfinished destiny of two heroes

The two heroes were following very different paths. The abnormal maiden accompanied Gawain from the outset and made him participate in many unexpected ventures as if she were trying to distract him from his initial destination. Meanwhile, Perceval was on the land for five years fighting against the knights that he encountered on his way, and all those he defeated he then ordered to go to King Arthur's castle. He knew they would do so because they feared him so much.

One Good Friday morning, a group of ladies and knights reproached the son of the 'Widowed Lady' for carrying weapons on such an important day. People had to repent of their sins. Convinced of his mistake, he decided to go and find a hermit saint. It turned out to be his uncle, who rebuked him for his mother's death, and later he revealed to him that the Grail was a *sacred object that produced a holy host, the only edible item that could sustain the Fisher King*, which was locked in the hall of the castle, where the beautiful damsels had appeared carrying the silver chopping board and the Grail.

During the last day that Perceval was at his uncle's side, he learnt a prayer that included many names for God, the greatest among them not to be pronounced on the lips of any man who was not in immediate danger of dying. The following morning the heroic knight went away. And the author of the 'romance' did not tell us what became of him.

Yet we do know of Gawain's escapades: in a revolving castle he fought against demons and was tended to by a mysterious 'queen with white plaits' called Ygerne, King Arthur's mother and his own grandmother, as Gawain was the monarch of Camelot's nephew. Some of the words of this noble royal knight, so articulate, were devoted to queen Guinevere:

Since the first woman was made from Adam's rib, there was nobody so famous… My queen and wife teaches and instructs everyone alive. The world's goodness comes from her, she is its source and origin…

"Le conte du Graal" came to an end when Gawain was taken prisoner in Ygerne's castle after suffering countless spells. He asked King Arthur for help and the messenger set off for Camelot. We do not know anything else as Chrétien de Troyes, the author, died suddenly, without resolving the situation. So the destiny of the two heroes was left unfinished.

Other authors took care to provide different endings in very similar works. In those times, using other writers' storylines was not considered to be plagiarism. They changed the outcome or modified the structure to introduce new characters or eliminate those that they considered to be in the way. They also took the trouble to replace almost all of the names.

Some of the symbols

Chrétien de Troyes peppered his work with symbols as it was aimed at a very limited public, belonging to the clergy and the educated sector of the nobility. These were times of wide-scale illiteracy when counts and dukes *were proud of the fact they could not read as they delegated this function to their closest servants*.

His Grail is comparable to the chalice of the Eucharist: *the host was the saintly object that nourished the Fisher King*. Perceval's mistake was not to ask the question in the room inside the castle after being stunned by the presence of the damsels carrying so many wonderful things; this meant that the hero must have been perfectly naïve, obedient to the orders of his elders, even though they made the mistake of imposing on him the discretion of not asking any questions, or 'knowing more than he needed'.

The bleeding spear could be a replica of the one that the centurion Longinus used to stab Jesus Christ in the side, although this is really an allegory of Celtic origin: the murder weapon wanted to give him away because it started bleeding in his presence. This reflects the guilt Perceval felt about his mother's death.

As for the damsel whose ring, meat pie and kiss he stole, she represents the world of temptations that was offered to the ignorant Perceval. If he had given in to them, he would have been trapped in an audacious spiral that would drive him to kill anyone who challenged the knights of the Round Table. He made a series of mistakes which was to culminate with the biggest of them all: not having asked the question at the time when he had the Grail in front of him.

Everything is found in the romance

"Le conte du Graal" had all the necessary ingredients to become the myth the Roman Church needed. The Pope was praising the Crusades. The fact that religion was waging war meant the commandment 'thou shall not kill' was being flouted after being obeyed since the Crucifixion, so belief in the Grail was given wings like a chimaera.

The Grail was the chalice of the Last Supper, the same one that Jesus Christ had taken in his hands. However it had already been found, or at least several countries thought so because they had it on their altars as their most highly prized religious jewel. It could also be something further... what if it had contained Jesus' blood after being taken down from the cross?

It was necessary to follow the development of the story when united to Joseph of Arimathea with the divine vessel. But it would take a little time for this character to be used. Before other versions of the Grail came out, most of them were based on "Le conte du Graal" by Chrétien de Troyes. Then the myth was repeatedly strengthened until it became a goal for knights.

In one of the storylines the knights alone had the true leading role. There were good and bad ones, the hero was increasingly idealized, almost an apostle of good and justice, and if he killed it was out of need. Was this not the message the Church aimed to convey by having backed the creation of the Order of the Temple or the Templars, whose members were warrior monks?

The desolate image of the failures

At this point we should mention the failures of the knights in their quest for the Grail as they far outnumbered their successes. When this happened, the image that it left was sterile. The barren moor was to be maintained and death was to continue acting as a harridan who enjoyed devastation; meanwhile, the

36

victims were awaiting the arrival of the hero who miraculously restored prosperity to that land. Because they needed a Paradise, although the sun no longer shone over Camelot as it had done previously.

The myth needed an image of devastation so that everything would burst with life upon the hero's triumph. But too many years of sadness had gone by. Could the past be fully recovered to the extent of cancelling out the memory of long years lived in darkness?

On many occasions the heroes in their quest for the Grail needed help from a number of angels, although this never guaranteed all out triumph.

Chapter III

THE 'PERCEVAL' OF WOLFRAM VON ESCHENBACH

An intentional influence

Wolfram von Eschenbach was a German poet, born in Bavaria during the thirteenth century. After serving Hermann of Thuringia, he died around 1217. He wrote several works, most of them unfinished, until he gave shape to *Perceval*, which should be regarded as a skilful adaptation of Chrétien de Troyes' *Le conte du Graal*. This poem warrants a close look because many historians believe it paved the way for the Grail myth to be accepted by the Roman Church and the nobility in continental Europe.

The novel *Perceval* begins with the adventures of Gahmuret in the East, when he placed his sword at the service of King Baruc of Baghdad. In one of the lulls in the continual wars he married a native who gave him a son named Vairefils. When he returned to the West he took up residence in Anjou, where he met a range of characters such as Uther Pendragon, King Arthur's father, the young Gawain and other heroes. In the end he married Herzeloyde and she was expecting before he returned to the East. The very same hour that his wife, in great pain, gave birth, he died in the midst of a gory battle. The child was to be named Perceval. The 'Widowed Lady' carefully educated him away from castles and knights, so destiny would not deal the same hand of cards to him as his father.

The meeting with three knights

When Perceval was young, he saw three knights riding through the wood pursuing Meleagent who had just abducted a lady. The young man was so curious that he followed them until he got them to tell him how they were armoured and the missions that they had to complete.

Perceval was so impressed that he begged his mother relentlessly to go to King Arthur's court, the 'Widowed Lady' gave way in the end, but not without first making him listen to her advice on safety; she dressed him like a jester so he would make people laugh wherever he went. Exceptionally, she gave him this warning before leaving:

The Knight of the Round Table had to aimlessly wander along paths and through woods in his quest to right wrongs or find the Grail chimaera.

Son of mine, you must be mindful that, despite your vassals, the bold and sober Le Hellin has seized two regions that you

should have inherited, Wales and Northern Wales. He also killed
your vassal Dorgental with his own hands, and he has beaten
your people and taken them prisoner.

These words made Perceval so furious that he did not hesitate in swearing to take revenge on his enemy by wounding him with his lance. He set out immediately without looking back despite hearing how his mother was dying of anguish.

As the young man was unaware of the effect that wearing a jester's suit could have, when he heard the jeers of the few people that he found along the way he did not know they were jeering at him. On reaching King Arthur's castle, once again he heard the jeers, but he was more interested in Queen Guinevere's suffering at the hands of Ithier of Gaheriez whom he eventually killed.

Perceval's training

Later, Perceval became skilled in the use of weapons under the old seneschal Gurnemanz of Graharz, the very person who knighted him a few years later. During his harsh training, the young man was attracted to his master's daughter, the beautiful Liase. They were about to marry but Perceval considered himself ready to go and satisfy his revenge, so he set out. However, he was tormented by the idea of not having found time to receive Liase's favours.

On arriving at the palace of the beautiful Condwiramur, he fell in love with her because she reminded him of the woman he had abandoned. This did not stop him from fighting against the enemies that besieged the territory and exterminating them. A while after, he resisted two nights of carnal temptations until on the third one he experienced love with a woman for the first time. However, he did not imagine that it was Liase, because the sensual Condwiramur was the one who had her arms around him.

The physical attraction the couple felt for each other became obsessive until Perceval remembered his destiny and decided to leave. It was a very painful parting for him especially as his love was down on her knees and would not stop crying as she tried to convince him to stay. Nothing weakens the hard heart of a person who wants to return to the land where he lived with his mother.

The 'Fisher King'

During his new journey, Perceval encountered the 'Fisher King' who was wearing a hat lined with peacock feathers. He invited Perceval to spend the night in the Grail castle where all the hearts of its dwellers knew only pain and suffering. However, the young knight was received in the highest luxury.

A squire suddenly crossed the threshold. He was carrying a spear that dripped blood from its tip and then ran down the shaft until it reached the carrier's hand to then be absorbed by his sleeve. The room was then drowned in moans and pleas. The squire circled the large room, carrying the morbid load until he reached the entrance and suddenly left, while at the far end a steel door opened and two noble-looking adolescents appeared... They were white virgins, and each was holding a gold candelabra with a burning candle. Behind them, the duchess was walking forward with her partner, he was carrying two marble pedestals, without wanting to waste any more time, others appeared also laden with objects: four carried flames and the remainder effortlessly held a precious stone that the sun shone through reflecting its brightness. Two ravishingly dressed princesses also appeared carrying two carving knives on an extraordinary white tray...They led the way for the queen. Her face was shining so brightly that it seemed like dawn was breaking. The essence of what was hoped to be found in paradise was brought in on an emerald green cushion: the Grail; it always surpassed anything a human being could imagine. Dispenser of Pleasure was the name of the maiden who was honoured with carrying the Grail...

Perceval's big mistake

Perceval was so taken aback by the wonders he was fortunate enough to witness that he made the big mistake of not asking the question. A little later when the lavish ceremony had finished they took him to some chambers. They continued to treat

him with great consideration, but this did not put him completely at his ease, so he slept badly.

The majestic nature of the Knights of the Holy Grail was evident
wherever they went.

The next morning, he found that the castle was completely
deserted. After crossing the drawbridge he found his horse saddled.
Before mounting, an invisible squire shouted this curse at him.

43

May the sun's scorn fall on you! You are a worm! You did not even take the trouble to open your mouth to ask your host...Having saved us all would have been a great credit to you!

The young knight pressed ahead, but was very disconcerted because he did not understand the meaning of the words he had just heard. A few hours later he found himself before a young girl kneeling beside the corpse of a boy. It turned out to be Sigune, a cousin of his, but he did not know her and she revealed the mystery of the Grail castle to him: if he had asked at the time during the ceremony...

Your grandfather, King Titurel, who was also known by the name of the 'Fisher King', would have been healed of all his wounds and then, prosperity would have been restored to those lands. But you absurdly kept quiet, something we all regret, the maiden continued. *Do not forget that your grandfather gave you a unique sword that will end up broken. As you will still need it, you will have to go in search of Trebuchet, the blacksmith, who lives close to the source of the lake, near Karmant. Only he can forge it...But you will not be able to return to Monsalvage, the Grail castle.*

Kundry 'the Witch'

Perceval continued on his way until once again he had before him the maiden whose meat pie and kiss had stolen. This time he repaired the damage done by achieving a sentimental commitment between her and the young Orilus, something that made the knight feel quite content.

However, the smile was wiped from his lips when he discovered bird blood stains on the snow. He got down from his horse and walked over to the red testimonies and knelt down... they reminded him so much of Condwiramur! As he refused to leave, several knights from King Arthur's court went to change his mind, each getting down from his horse prompted by Perceval. It was the only answer he gave them.

He did not do the same with Gawain, the great public speaker, who got on his horse and rode away from where the blood stains had disappeared hours before. Once Perceval was in

Camelot, he received good news: Queen Guinevere had pardoned him for killing Ithier of Gaheriez. That helped him to live with himself for a few weeks, which turned out to be moments of fun, until the ugly damsel on the mule appeared, called Kundry 'the Witch…'

She had a mastiff's nose. Two boar's teeth that were an inch long came out of her mouth and her eyebrows stood on end and met her hairline…Her ears were like those of a bear. Her grim face did not invite the caresses of a lover…That person lacking in human kindness walked on monkey legs and her nails were as sharp as a lion's…She also wore a hat made of peacock feathers and brandished a whip with silk straps and a ruby inlaid handle. Her whole appearance made her look like the queen of the animals…

Suddenly, Kundry started to insult Perceval, then she spoke to him about his father Gatimuret and Vairefils, his brother, finishing in the following way:

By just uttering one word in Monsalvage you could have made yourself the owner of more riches than are kept in Tabronita, the pagan city that your brother Vairefils, the 'Angevin', captured from the black queen of Sazamanca.

As the Knights of the Round Table had overheard 'the Witch', they got the impression that there was a place full of treasure and they decided to go and look for it. Perceval also went but his sword broke after coming out victorious in a hard-fought battle. This prompted him to go and seek the help of the hermit Trevrizent.

How the Earth ceased to be virgin

The hermit was apparently expecting him. After serving him food and drink, he led him through to where a bed awaited him. During the night Perceval woke up, lucid, and heard a series of explanations that were to lead him to the universe of the Grail:

When Lucifer sank with his retinue to hell, God replaced him with a man: he took some earth and made noble Adam from it. From Adam's body he made Eve…From these two beings, children were born; one of them, due to unchecked pride, eventual-

ly sullied his grandmother, who was still a virgin. Many people, before understanding the meaning of these words, are surprised and asked how could such a thing happen.

Perceval asked the hermit to explain the mystery to him, and he continued with the account:

Adam's mother was the Earth and he lived off her fruits. In those times the Earth was still virgin. But I have not told you who took away her virginity. Adam was the father of Cain and he killed Abel in a miserable attack of jealousy. Therefore Adam's son took the virginity...

The young man listened without understanding very clearly. However, he was aware of the message he was being given which would turn out to be very useful. He endeavoured to understand and, in the end, he did.

The essence of the Grail

Slowly, Trevrizent's explanations took other directions in order to approach the essence of the Grail.

Thoughts are capable of stealing themselves away from the sun's gaze; thoughts, although no lock contains them, remain hidden, impenetrable to any creature; thoughts are the darkness where no light penetrates. But divinity has the power to illuminate everything: its brightness radiates through the wall that surrounds darkness...all this is accomplished by the Grail, the power of God, but it must act like a waterfall, the 'pure brother' on becoming 'Perfect'...The Grail that you saw in the Castle of Monsalvage was under the protection of the Templars, that often ride off on their horses in search of adventure. The results of their fights are not important; whether they end in glory or humiliation they accept them with a serene heart, taking it as atonement for their sins...

The food the Templars eat comes from a precious stone that is, in essence, totally pure. If you do not know it I will tell you its name: it is called Lapsit exilis. The phoenix is consumed and turns into ashes on account of its qualities, but from these ashes life is reborn and thanks to the stone, the phoenix then reappears in all its splendour, as beautiful as ever. There is no man ill enough not to escape from death within a week of seeing the stone. Whoever sees it does not grow old. From the day the stone appears to them, all men and all women recover their appearance from when they were in full health. Were they to be in the presence of the stone for two hundred years, they would not change, except for their hair turning grey. That stone makes a man so vigorous that his bones and flesh recover their youth instantly. It is also called Grail... Every Good Friday the stone is as good as to provide the best potions and the finest delicacies...furthermore, the stone provides its guardians with all types of game...

I will tell you that on the edge of the stone there is a mysterious description with the names and descent of those destined to complete this ill-fated quest to find it. There is no need to scratch the inscription off as it disappears before the eyes of the beholder as soon as he sees his name. The chosen ones may be found in distant lands or right here...

A noble brotherhood resides in the castle of Montsalvage. The members have fought bravely to prevent impure people getting close to the Grail, except for those whose names are written on one of the edges of the divine stone. This is how the Grail manifests its esoteric nature: nobody can enter the sanctuary that has not been chosen magically. Nobody can see there Amfortas, the 'Fisher King' you met, because he did not keep his vow of chastity as he went in search of a love, that is why he was wounded in his manhood with a poisoned spear.

Now I will speak to you about the Grail's descent. Grandfather Titurel had a son, King Frimutel, who died leaving behind him several descendants: my sister Josiane, the bearer of the Grail and Dispenser of Pleasure, Amfortas, Herzeloyde, your mother and myself...although it hurts me, I must tell you that your mother died of sorrow on seeing you depart...a tragedy that you should not lament too much because your destiny was already written; find King Le Hellin because he killed the Knight of the Grail and he stole the white horse Guengalet, that we called Gringalet. Then he murdered your own mother and my sister, indirectly...

Perceval was impatient to discover what his destiny was. He knew everything he had just been told was true and he was ready to assume his responsibilities. Trevizent the hermit stopped him however because he needed to tell him something very important:

Do not try to go without knowing the mistake you made in the Grail castle: you should have asked the 'Fisher King' this question: what suffering have you fallen victim to?

The witches may have been allies of the Knights of the Grail rather than the incarnation of their worst enemies.

Gawain and the sorcerer Klingsor

At this point in the novel, Wolfram von Eschenbach leaves Perceval to tell us of Gawain's adventures. He reached Castle Marvel, which was owned by the sorcerer Klingsor, a very cruel character who subjected the knight to different challenges, some almost deadly. He was dying when the Flower-Girls rescued him. They only retained him long enough to save him because Gawain needed to reach the city of the thousand treasures.

No sooner had he set out than he was confronted with other challenges, until he came to the Dangerous Ford. Once he had managed to complete the challenge he found out that his mysterious enemy, sorcerer Klingsor, was actually the former Duke of Mantua, who the king had ordered to be castrated for having seduced his wife. As revenge, the adulterer devoted all his time to studying the most diabolical arts in order to make prisoners of all the ladies and gentlemen that passed by the castle. However, he had imposed one condition on himself that he may never have thought about fulfilling as he believed it to be impossible: surrender to the one who overcame every single one of the challenges created by his magic.

As Gawain had just come out of the last test at the Dangerous Ford unscathed, Klingsor the sorcerer had no choice but to release all the male and female prisoners that filled his castle's dungeons. Surprisingly, among the released were King Arthur's mother, and Gawain's mother and sister.

Weeks later, after passing by Camelot, Gawain jousted constantly with a mysterious knight for two days. When both adversaries were on the ground, weakened but with their swords in hand prepared to continue fighting they asked each other's name. Before speaking they lifted their helmets, which enabled them to recognise each other: they were Gawain and Perceval.

They recognised the fact that they could not beat one another and then embraced each other laughing. After having water and something to eat they took some time to rest.

The Witch's prophesy

The two knights continued to rise to the challenges that the great adventures imposed until Gawain exchanged the quest for the city of a thousand treasures for marriage: he wed the beautiful Orgelus. This deeply saddened Perceval as it had brought back memories of Condwiramur to him. He ended up travelling until he came across a black-skinned knight wearing oriental clothes. They fought hard until the sword that belonged to the fair-skinned knight broke. His rival then dropped his weapons and said his name: Vairefils, 'the Angevin'.

Suddenly, Perceval remembered that was his step-brother's name, that is, the son his father had with the princess of Orient. They embraced and afterwards spoke about members of their family, living or dead. Subsequently, they rode to King Arthur's castle.

The next day, Kundry appeared there again, 'the Witch' who stood in Perceval's way; yet on this occasion she did not do it to insult him but so he would listen to her prophesy:

An inscription has appeared on the divine stone which orders you to become the king of the Grail. Condwiramur, your wife, and your son Lohengrin, will be called to the castle with you…What I have announced is also written in the stars, as well knows the noble and rich Vairefils, your black stepbrother, who is now on your right.

The two brothers, one white and the other black, pledged themselves to conquering the Grail castle. They made this decision by posing themselves a key question. By that time Perceval had already married Condwiramur and had two twin sons, Kardeis and Lohengrin, but he did not know them as they were born while he was in the Waste Land. When the ceremony was celebrated in the Grail castle, the white knight was able to see the divine stone; however the black knight was deprived of this honour on account of his being pagan. Yet he could look at the Dispenser of Pleasure who was the bearer of the object that gave eternal life.

Vairefils was christened the following day so he could marry the Dispenser of Pleasure. Together they immediately headed East after saying goodbye to their friends and family.

Incidentally, we know that this couple had a son who was to be the famous Father John.

Beyond the 'racist' message of *Perceval*

The opinion that Jean Markale offers in his work *Le cycle du Graal* about the storyline of the novel that we have extracted in this chapter is of particular interest:

Perceval *is a very dense, involved account, full of flowery padding, astrological considerations and commentaries inspired by neo-platonic thought and oriental traditions. We have still to determine the personal contribution of Wolfram von Eschenbach to this epic. It is very possible that the oriental elements that fill* Perceval *are taken from his model, but certainly not from Chrétien de Troyes. He unquestionably preserved the primitive framework of the quest, the one that is more Celtic, but he modifies it considerably through his interpretations. What is also clear is that he wanted to make the story more oriental; that is what is behind Vairefils' role, and above all, his leaving for the Orient with Dispenser of Pleasure. This way, the elements taken from the Orient return there and the Grail became one of the great mythical-legendary frameworks that reconciled two apparently diametrically opposed worlds.*

It cannot be denied that the Grail itself occupies a secondary role in Perceval. *The Templars, guardians of the Grail and holders of a secret tradition, seem to be more important. It also seems that initiating the search takes priority over the purely mystical aspect as he does not reach Monsalvage through an ascesis but a mysterious designation has occurred through letters that appear on the Grail-Stone. As guardian of the Grail one is not only a priest but also a warrior. Did Wolfram reconcile spiritual man with natural man? There is no doubt whatsoever. He put the following words in Kundry's mouth when he spoke to Perceval: "Have you attained peace of mind and have you waited for your body's happiness through a faithful desire?" (an allusion to the hero's fidelity towards his wife Condwiramur). But at what price is the harmony between these two fundamental tendencies of the human being obtained? Here is where everything becomes ambiguous and even dangerous.*

A maiden with King Arthur. Miniature taken from a French manuscript conserved at the National Library of Paris.

And the elitism manifest in 'Perceval' is much more obvious than in other versions of the quest for the Grail. This elitism means that a magic decision or prediction was first necessary. The character of Galahad could only have been chosen in this way, in the Cistercian quest for the Grail. All the other participants in the search tried their luck and it was not beyond anyone's bounds. We can see how, from the notion of the elitist choice of the fraternity of the Templars, priests and warriors, receivers of a secret and sacred tradition, some theorists could fuel their fantasies about 'a pure race', 'a chosen race' and other aberrations, that unfortunately have prompted wars, massacres, genocide and 'final solutions'. It would be ridiculous if

this were not a pure tragedy and also if some of our contempo-
raries, nostalgic for a state of mind that we thought had been
overcome, did not find in the Grail and through Wolfram von
Eschenbach an additional reason to believe in biological deter-
minism. Yet this is what happens in all great works, they contain
the seed of numerous children that do not always resemble one
another.

A brief clarification

Jean Markale is referring to Hitler and Nazism because they
took inspiration from books like *Perceval* and others to preach
the pureness of race that would do so much harm to the whole
of mankind. Incidentally, the Nazis believed in the existence of
the Grail to such an extent that they commissioned Otto Rahn
(the author of a magnificent work, albeit controversial, about
the relationship between the Grail and Catharism) to go off to
the Pyrenees to find it. They took advantage of the fact that they
had just conquered France in the first years of the Second World
War to do so.

Rahn did not find the Grail, however, although he was able
to greatly broaden his knowledge about the Cathars and their
influence, as in those years they could still be found in the
regions of the Pyrenees (a book, incidentally, has been published on this interesting subject in this collection).

It is worth emphasizing that *Perceval* is something more than
an elitist message, capable of fuelling racist ideas, as all the way
through it offers a deep sense of spirituality. Given that it included many positive aspects of Christianity, it helped to promote
the myth of the Grail, especially in Central Europe. One of the
best examples is the opera *Parsifal* by Richard Wagner, the title
of this opera should be interpreted as a variant of Perceval.

Some of the symbols

Under the surface of the poem of *Perceval* looms the mystery of the Trinity: Man, Woman and Nature as God's creations.
All are subject to an inescapable condition: ageing. However,

just as in Nature, what grows old to die makes way for a new life in a short cycle, man and woman have the vehicle of love to reproduce. When Perceval found his wife in the same place as where blood had fallen on the ground, his passion was greatly strengthened. Later, he met Trevizent, who said something of great importance:

I lament your futile effort because history had never supposed that man could conquer the Grail. I would have pulled your hand away very quickly; but through you there was another opportunity. We do not regret what has happened because you will receive another nobler prize.

What the hermit is trying to say is that if the hero was unsuccessful in his endeavour to conquer the Grail physically, he should not be sorry because he has attained a spiritual victory, as he passed all the tests for many years until reaching the peak. His values of mercy, tolerance and love were sufficient. Certainly, he lacked the absolute pureness preventing the Grail from revealing all its secrets to him, yet he was far from bearing a grudge, he was still the same, nobody could take away from him, at least from an internal assessment, the merit of still considering himself a hero.

On the other hand, many aspects of the Grail, so different on so many occasions, make it very clear that we are faced with one of the most famous enigmas of all medieval times. A literary subject had never excited the imagination so much of anyone who made it their objective to find out what was hiding behind the veil of appearances. A sacred object had never been searched for yet feared so much.

It was the chalice that illuminated the night with unreal light that millions of human beings, in search of the truth, longed to find. Without exaggerating, the Grail was comparable to the alchemists' philosopher's stone, which everyone talked about but no-one had ever seen. Who was to be the hero brave and prudent enough to go into the dark leafiness of Broceliande wood, in search of a castle, the wood being guarded by a 'Fisher King' who was weak and in need of being rescued in all senses despite the fact that this could have led to his own death?

Questions spring to mind concerning the followers of this myth, as they knew that behind the adventures that shaped it were hidden symbols relating to the existence of all human beings. Living is already a path of sorts in the quest to find the Grail because we do not know the real mission we are here to fulfil in this world. We also do not know what the sentence of having to die responds to, maybe in the midst of illness or after not having had the opportunity to succeed. That is why we need to believe in something, to have an objective. Surely deep down we know that *we should not wish on anybody what we do not wish for ourselves*, and with this we can function, as our Grail is solidarity.

Obviously we are talking about a myth, something supernatural as it forms part of the dreams that are out of reach; but each one of us needs to believe that they can be touched, even if only through literature.

Chapter IV
JOSEPH OF ARIMATHEA

Everything began after Calvary

Curiously, the four evangelists cited Joseph of Arimathea as the man who helped take Jesus' body down from the cross and subsequently to the tomb. Such agreement is rarely found, as when narrating the birth in Bethlehem for example the same version is not told.

Joseph of Arimathea was thought to be an important member of the Sanhedrin in Jerusalem and he was frequently in contact with Pontius Pilot. This is why he was granted permission to bury one of the crucified people, which was an exception as corpses of the condemned were usually thrown into common graves.

Apparently, Joseph deposited Jesus' body onto a sort of stretcher. His intention was to wash the corpse and then cover it with linen. When he was doing the first task some drops of blood seeped out of his spear wound in his side that the eminent Jew was careful to collect in a cup or chalice. As he was carrying several recipients of this type, some of them contained ointments and aromatic oils and others were empty, so he may have used one of the empty ones.

According to another version of the legend, Joseph of Arimathea was arrested for having stolen Jesus' body after a group of Pharisees had found the tomb empty. While he was in the cell, the Resuscitated appeared to him surrounded by light. Jesus already considered him to be his apostle, and handed him the chalice of the Grail from the Last Supper with a few drops of blood. His next act was to instruct him, in few words, on how mass was to be held in the future, telling him of the Incarnation and other mysteries relating to the Resurrection.

Joseph of Arimathea supposedly took the chalice from the last supper from Jerusalem to Britain.

Joseph had taken on great responsibility and was rewarded on a daily basis: even though the prison warders did not give him food or water, he could nourish himself with the host that a dove left for him every morning in the miraculous chalice. He apparently spent more than twenty years in prison. When he was released his sister and brother Bron were waiting for him. Together they escaped from the country.

Where did they really go?

All three of them went to different cities in the Mediterranean by boat and subject to harassment by the Romans they reached the island of Britain. There, under the influence of the Grail that Joseph of Arimathea still had with him, they decided to build a big circular table, the forerunner to the Round Table, which twelve people could sit round. They left one seat free, the eleventh, in memory of Jesus or Judas.

It proved true that anyone that sat on the eleventh seat ended up disappearing. They called it the 'Siege Perilous'. After a few months, the Jews travelled to Glastonbury where they built a church in honour of the Mother of Jesus. They placed the Grail on the altar. This attracted many of the faithful to the location, and in the end, they built an abbey after Joseph of Arimathea and his brother and sister had died.

The third legend described how Joseph of Arimathea handed the Grail to his brother Bron who was to be known as the Splendid Fisherman, thanks to his being able to feed a hundred of his followers with the fish he took from the Grail. These people then looked for shelter in a place called Avaron or Avalon.

In time they managed to erect a temple in Muntsalvache or Mount Saviour where the order of the Grail knights was established, their only mission being to conserve and protect such a sacred vessel. Masses and other religious ceremonies that centred on the Grail were organized and performed by a priest. When he was mysteriously injured by a burning spear in the legs, piercing him very close to the male organs, he became known as the Mutilated King. At the same time, the land that surrounded the temple became barren causing it to become known as the Waste Land. The spear that injured the priest was believed to be similar to the one that the centurion Longinus had thrust into Jesus Christ's side.

This is how the four objects relating to the Grail took shape: the chalice, the spear, a stone fountain and the sword that only the 'sublime hero' could wield, although the risk of breaking due to misuse always hung heavily over it.

Some tombs, an abbey and a novel

According to historical records, in 1190 the tombs of King Arthur and Guinevere were at Glastonbury. That is where an abbey was built and the monks took care to promote King Arthur's myth, and for it they used the novel *Perlesvaus,* which is another of the many variants of the *Romance of Perceval* or *Le conte du Graal.* However, in this case the young man setting out was neither naïve nor ignorant. He had to avenge his father and recover the family properties. He was to achieve this goal but not without spilling a lot of blood.

In essence, *Perlesvaus* retraces Perceval's trail until he reached the Grail castle. At this point the mistake concerning not asking a question did not only condemn the 'Fisher King' but also affected the king of Camelot, whose court had been abandoned as he could no longer do favours and had lost his power to protect its members. However Guinevere reacted by asking her husband to go on a pilgrimage to the chapel of Saint Augustus in Wales.

King Arthur could not enter the chapel, although he was already at its doors. While he was contemplating it from the outside he had a holy vision. On his return he was forced to fight with a knight wielding a bright sword. His gut reaction was to flee because he thought he had lost his powers; however, he ended up fighting as he saw that all his escape routes were closed. He eventually won the combat, which made him realise that he had recovered all his old powers and, in addition his power to do favours.

He established his new court in Penzance in Cornwall where he received the emissaries of the Fisher King. They told him about the menaces that had devastated the regions where the

Grail Castle was and before leaving they gave him the shield that had belonged to Joseph of Arimathea.

This is how the evangelistic character that took Jesus Christ down from the cross appeared in the novel. No other author had used this name so closely linked to the most mysterious area of land of the Resurrection. Its inclusion gave the abbey at Glastonbury one of the last elements it needed to immortalize the myth of the Grail and at the same time the whole universe relating to King Arthur and the Round Table.

The Roman Church already had what it was looking for, as all chivalrous novels that were to be written would fuel the idea that it was *impossible to get due revenge without enemy blood flowing*. The message was closely linked to the Crusades that the European kings had to continually reinforce by sending their best knights to the Holy Land.

Curiously, the Roman Church very rarely used the word Grail officially as if its origin were pagan. The Church was concerned about how much violence the knights employed; their aggression always had to be channelled into a 'just cause'. That is why it supported duels of honour, tournaments, which were called 'judgements of God' and all military ceremonies that played to his interests. In that period not a sword moved without looking to Rome, in search of papal backing.

Avalon or the 'White Island'

The writer Robert de Boron sited Avalon in Great Britain, where Joseph of Arimathea arrived with some of his followers, notably, Alano and Petrus. The latter had a vocation to go to Avalon, the 'White Island', as it was 'where his heart called him'. There he waited for somebody who knew how to read the divine letter he was carrying so he could then announce himself to be the true power of the Grail.

According to the legend, Joseph of Arimathea was buried in Avalon. Its cemetery became the perfect resting place for all the heroes with a Grail connection because they had to cross the water miraculously, just as Jesus' apostle did. If they had kept themselves pure they would float even when they ran out of energy, as the distance was a long one to cover: if they were carrying sins, however, they would sink even if they were the world's strongest swimmers.

Old painting showing the moment when the 'Fisher King' was injured in the thigh by a mysterious character.

To Wolfram Von Eschenbach, another of the great writers that forged the literary myth on the Grail, Avalon is where King Mazadan was to be found, as he had been taken to Feimurgan by Ter-de-la-Schoye, a supernatural woman. This character is still the Morgan from the Arthurian cycle, and she lived in the 'Land of Pleasure', one of the names given to Britain by the Celts.

Robert de Boron, who also belonged to the creators of a character similar to Perceval, described how his hero, Parsifal, found out that the 'Fisher King', a name often given to Joseph of Arimathea himself, was his real father and that he was *in a far off country in the West where the sun sets (Avalon)*. There he was to remain while his son performed sufficient heroic acts to allow him to become the champion of all knights.

The holy oil of Joseph of Arimathea

Robert de Boron saw Joseph of Arimathea as a 'noble knight' as he had lent his great services to Pontius Pilate for seven years. That is why he accepted his request as soon as he had he formulated it to take care of the Crucified's body. Later in the tomb, he collected the drops of blood in the Grail. As he was considered a tomb-robber he was imprisoned *in a house similar to a hollow pillar in the middle of a pantheon*. Thanks to the miraculous chalice he managed to withstand forty years in prison.

Once released, he was baptized by Christians and Jesus himself, using holy oil, ordained him as the first bishop. As Jesus left him some of this oil, Joseph of Arimathea took it to Britain where he was to ordain all the kings of this country, even Uther Pendragon, King Arthur's father.

All this points to a part of Christianity reaching Britain, where it was strengthened through the Grail myth and the Arthurian cycle without the Roman Church playing an important role. It nevertheless allowed for the faith preached by Jesus to be consolidated in a country where Celtic influence was so dominant.

When Joseph of Arimathea reached the 'White Island', it could well have been undergoing a long period of material and spiritual poverty. As the presence of the apostle made prosperity appear, the religiousness that had come from the South was thought be an infinite power. It was therefore associated with the Grail's power to wipe out the negative spells that weighed over the country, and as some thought, over the world.

The Church aimed to ignore it

Despite how consolidated Christianity in Great Britain had become thanks to the Grail, the Roman Church seemed to be unaware of the fact. In 1898, E. Weschler wrote:

Despite its decidedly religious character, the Grail legend was not recognized by the Church or by the clergy. No religious writer made reference to the Grail. In religious literature that has reached us, nowhere do we find the name of the Grail, it is not even mentioned, with the exception of the chronicler Elinando. However, these authors could not have been ignorant to the marvellous account that symbolized faith. Rather, they must have cast a spell of silence around the myth.

J. Marx shared this opinion: *the Church never claimed the legend of the Grail for itself. Seemingly, it saw something in it of a primordial, original, or mysterious nature.*

This could be due to the Grail having too many esoteric symbols. Many authors drew parallels between the chalice and the Eucharist while specialists rejected the idea; they conceived the myth as an initiation. This explains why Robert de Boron wrote the following:

This story is a valuable one and cannot be told to people incapable of understanding it, as every good thing told to evil men will never be learnt by them. They are not primed to understand it and any effort or attempt in doing so is on a par with throwing flowers to pigs.

Those who saw the myth from its most sublime angle believed that the authentic book of the Grail was written by Jesus himself and then transmitted mentally to the person who was to transcribe it. This suggests the reader first had to undergo a purifying initiation process. The precaution had to be taken because while reading, apparitions could occur, and the unfortunate reader's spirit could be snatched away by the angels to be taken to where the Holy Trinity is found and opening the case that contained the Holy Grail meant entering in direct contact with Jesus Christ.

The theme that constantly runs through its powers, including its healing ones, commitment, heroic ventures, and the permanent quest for the Grail, is the infinite notion of the mystery, which has absolutely nothing to do with the Paradise promised to the purest Christians.

That anonymous author

The anonymous author of *Perlesvaus* is worthy of a section as he took the work *Joseph of Arimathea* by Robert de Boron to christianise it even more. He was thought to be a chaplain in an aristocratic house in Belgium or the north of France. He must have been an important person, as he had access to one of the few libraries in that period where he could read works on the Grail. This deduction has been made in light of the knowledge he demonstrated on this subject.

He contributed material of Welsh origin to the legend, conferring a macabre atmosphere to the text that combined the Celtic universe with Christian devotion. The work *Perlesvaus* could be said to bring together the pagan core and elements exclusive to the Roman Church. He must have written it between 1192 and 1225, as it reflects the influence of the Crusades, especially the ease with which swords were used to spill blood. At the same time, the hero expressed, not even slightly ashamed, that he was ready to kill any pagan not willing to embrace the New Order.

The anonymous author states in the first pages of his book that the storyline was taken from another, written in Latin that he had found in a blessed house on the island of Avalon in the Hazardous Marshlands. The abbey of Glastonbury was erected in the south-west of Great Britain, which is where scholars had identified the origin of the Holy Grail. Even though this anonymous author knew this site, he was not believed to have participated in the campaign to sanctify it.

Yet the Church still did not react

In *Perlesvaus,* a monk intervenes in the legend to endow it with more Christian elements. Soaked in the atmosphere of the time, the author's work was heavily charged with violence. This may be one of the bloodiest stories that reached Europe; killings were being 'authorized' in the Holy Land, the justification being the recovery of Jerusalem and other lost territories.

The Roman Church still did not react officially. They were glad that poems, novels and chivalrous novels on the Grail had acquired variants and reasonably so: yet it was committed to another crusade on mainland Europe against the Cathars, who were related to the Grail through a different channel to the church. It had to be very careful in supporting such a dangerous legend.

Chapter V
KING ARTHUR

The 'most fearsome bear man'

King Arthur belongs to the historical characters that have been modelled by legend rather than by reality. He was believed to be the son of Uther Pendragon, and his character offered Celtic and Hyperborean influences. He fought against the Anglo-Saxons between the fifth and sixth centuries. However, this incomplete biographical information must not let us lose sight of the main idea; namely he was a supreme representative, another type of royalty or sovereignty that we may consider to be universal.

This idea came from the Celts, who regarded Gods as kings because they put their lives, estates and will in their hands. They obeyed these Gods to the point of annulling their own opinion and judgement with the proviso that this submission brought them victory, riches and good governance. However, in the face of a notorious defeat or several years of bad harvests or long plagues, they expected these knights to commit suicide or, at least, hand themselves over to the enemy in order to save the survivors, especially the elderly, women and children.

Since King Arthur became the central axis of novels and poems on the Grail, he ceased to belong to England or Britain to become, during the Middle Ages, a supranational myth. He was the monarch of Western chivalry, therefore of all medieval Europe. Apparently, the dream of any young noble man was to become a member of the mythical order of the Round Table.

By the same token, the name Arthur offers different interpretations, the most authorized of which being the one that draws on the Celtic terms *arthos*: bear and *viros*: man. Nemius simplified it in the following way: *Arthur in Latin sounds like the 'most terrible bear'*. This meaning introduces us to an exceptional human being of fear-inspiring virile strength and a sacred quality.

Merlin, the magician who protected King Arthur, was an almost spectral being whose great powers conferred an immortal character on him.

In effect, in the old Celtic cult, just like in the most primitive astronomy, the 'Great Bear' of polar constellation is mentioned. Celestial symbols closely linked to the old Thule, that was the primitive name for Britain, the fabulous 'White Island' of the Hyperboreans. As we see, King Arthur united two magic elements: the 'polar' and the regal.

What Merlin represented

Since childhood, Arthur's destiny was inextricably linked to that of the magician Merlin whose origins are not explained by anyone. It is held that he was aged over sixty or seventy so he could still walk upright and live alone. Nobody knew as much as him, especially in the sphere of mystery and concealment. But he was a kind-hearted sort of superior druid.

He definitely led Arthur the young boy by the hand while he taught him the secrets of life and knowledge, among which the bad ones outstripped the good. Nothing was left out, as he resorted to the almost impossible on account of the fact that a king was exposed to thousands of different pressures.

Arthur was not to leave Merlin's side even when he was appointed king, his sovereignty being both material and spiritual. This double concept that was extended to the group of knights accompanying him and shaped the Round Table as they were not only warriors, as Thomas Malory relates in *Le Morte d'Arthur*:

They all felt more blessed and worthy of veneration than if they had conquered half the World. That is why they did not stop to think about leaving their wives, children and families to comply with the rules of the Order with all the material and spiritual power they possessed.

There is no doubt that the Order of the Round Table was a religion of sorts which was entirely confused with the Grail. It would have been similar to the Order of the Temple if the Templars had not wanted to wrest the Holy Land from the sons of Islam, and the predominance these sons exercised over the Holy Sepulchre they considered to be an embarrassment to Christianity.

The power of magic

There is a beautiful legend connected to the stones at Stonehenge and Merlin. Apparently, Merlin gave orders to some warriors to extract a hundred gigantic stones from a quarry, which were then going to be used to build a large solar temple. He told them, *Get to work, brave men, by bringing down those stones you will learn that the spirit is always stronger than force*. But many warriors were not capable of doing the work no matter how hard they tried and in the end Merlin must have done it alone using nothing but his magic or his spirit. Through some kind of cabalistic sentences and hand movements that only he knew, in other words, the stones flew out of the quarry, completely cut and placed themselves in the position that can still be seen today in the solar temple of Stonehenge.

The legend does not seem to fit in with historical dates as we now know that this impressive archaeological testimony dates back to the Megalithic or Neolithic period having supposedly been made by some giants that were alive in that period.

To the Knights of the Round Table, spirituality took precedence over the material world, as this was the only way they could perform their most astonishing heroic deeds. The following was read to them: *Fight for your land and accept death if necessary, as death is a victory and a freeing of the soul*. Here we find the old concept of a 'victorious death' which is so frequent in the heroes of Greek and Roman mythology.

The meaning of Excalibur

According to legend, Arthur was recognised as the legitimate king of all England because he had managed to draw a sword from the large quadrangular stone it was wedged in that stood in front of the altar in the temple. It is thought to be a variant of the 'stone of the kings' belonging to the sagas that originated from the north of Germania: Siegfried passed a similar test by pulling a sword out of the 'magic tree', which nobody else could manage.

Specialists suggest that in this Arthurian sequence there are two very characteristic symbols: first, the fundamental stone which granted a title of greatness to whoever succeeded and second, the sword which was pulled out of something material to then take on spiritual importance.

Merlin had already announced to Arthur that he would receive the crown of England when he made the sword Excalibur or Caliburn his. The weapon had been forged in Avalon from where only superior things derived, and not only in a material capacity.

That is why Merlin advised King Arthur to shape the Round Table which in the long run was to become one of the supreme symbols of Camelot. The castle was separated from the outside world by a wide and ever-fast flowing river. A bridge needed to be crossed to get over the river and it could only be done by those who wore their honours as taught. Knights on guard threw all those that were unworthy into the water.

The Round Table

It would appear that the Round Table was made using the universe as a reference, including both the sky and the Earth. Given that it was always in action, it was like a centrepiece, around which the ever-dynamic knights sat. There were twelve of them because the Earth had been divided into a similar number of parts and each had a king. We also should see the 'twelve' as a solar figure that has occupied an important place since far off times. Examples are the twelve Olympic gods, the twelve Palatine Counts of Charlemagne, the twelve signs of the zodiac, etc.

One of the Round Table's oddities was that one seat was reserved for a predestined knight. The so-called 'Siège Perilous' could have been the eleventh or the thirteenth. The legend tells us that when King Arthur imposed the existence of the 'Siège Perilous' on Merlin's advice, when he had just started his quest for the Grail. England had just started to be known as the 'White

Island'. These were times of decadence when spiritual regeneration was needed, and this divine object could recover the splendid past.

The Round Table was always presided by the empty Siège Perilous. On this occasion Merlin attended the meeting.

The Grail must therefore be appreciated as *what had been lost and needed to be recovered as soon as possible*. This made King Arthur into a supra-historic person found at the centre of all events, be they tragic or noble. He still turned out to be very vulnerable, however, and this is shown by the fact that three characters tried to take Guinevere, his wife, away from him. The first was Maelvas, who took her to the town of Glastonbury, the second was his nephew Modred and the third was Sir Lancelot of the Lake. But this is worthy of a chapter to itself.

Modred's betrayal

King Arthur had abandoned England in his wish to broaden his domains. When he reached Rome itself he was informed that his nephew Modred had betrayed him. He had dared to kidnap Guinevere, so King Arthur had to return. This is how a very bloody war was triggered in which the traitor died along with several of the best knights of the Round Table. Arthur himself was also seriously injured.

He was quickly taken to Avalon, so the women of that land could heal him, Morgan, the one who was 'born of the sea' was their leader. They only partially healed King Arthur's wounds as they were to open on a yearly basis on account of their being caused by a spear that, besides being poisoned, had been cursed with an indestructible spell.

A lady was always present in Arthurian and Grail legends, especially queens. They were capable of enflaming the most exacerbated passions.

When King Arthur was actually dead and buried, his follow-ers still hoped that he would return from beyond the grave to regenerate England. The throne remained empty for a long time. In one of the most beautiful legends, Arthur's uncorrupted body was described as if he were sleeping placidly in a crystal castle erected on the top of a snow-capped mountain.

According to the official version, Arthur was buried in Glastonbury Abbey where his remains were united with those of Queen Guinevere. That is why the Grail myth and the whole fantastic cycle of Arthurian poems, romances and novels derive from there.

The myth was one that immortalized a king that could never have existed, as we will demonstrate in the following chapters, by citing authors that claim that King Arthur is a symbol or a 'literary nickname' for counts and kings from Spain and other countries.

Chapter VI

THE GRAIL COULD HAVE REACHED THE PYRENEES

The essence of the Grail

The Grail could be a cup, a glass or a precious stone. Christian legend tried to make people believe that it was a vessel — this is how we shall refer to it, with no pejorative intention, as we do not know its real form — used by Jesus Christ at the Last Supper, and the one that Joseph of Arimathea used to collect his Master's blood after his crucifixion. In actual fact, it was a mystery, a goal to be achieved, just as the source of eternal youth is sought after, or the alchemists who dreamt of the philosopher's stone while working on their distillations and retorts.

Several heterodox historians locate the Grail in lands of Manes, the founder of Manicheanism, while others attributed it to the Celts, as they represented sovereignty with a caldron, a plate, or a cup from 'the great beyond'.

Christian legend was based on Jesus Christ's disciples being persecuted, so any garment or object that could identify them had to hidden. They could never be sure that their chosen hideout would not be vulnerable in the long run, and if the person guarding it was being harassed, the Grail was taken somewhere else. Until, that is, it was taken to a mysterious castle possibly located in the Pyrenees or England, forever!

Where the legend acquired its greatest beauty

The Anglo-Saxons claimed the Grail legend for themselves, but confused it with the legend of the Round Table and the 'Arthurian' stories relating to King Arthur of England. On reaching this point a hero should emerge, which is only logical for any story aiming to become immortal.

Leaving aside the historian's objectivity, it is tempting to play with the literature, but our intention is not to misrepresent the legend. The twelfth seat at the Round Table, the so-called 'Siège Perilous' was always vacant... Who would occupy it? Was it such an unattainable enterprise?

A fascinating legend

The legend takes its base from several mythologies, including Homer's "Odyssey" and other stories. But we can deduce that ourselves. The troubadours expressed the legend, swore by its authenticity and seemingly, they were believed. They were also copied, as a series of stories with similar characteristics appeared and were to span the remainder of the Middle Ages. They were even to arouse the curiosity of 'the madman', Don Quixote de La Mancha.

Yet the legend of Perceval or the Grail was impregnated with elements that tempted the mind, made the heart passionate and the soul shudder. The hero's origin was a bitter one, but this did not prevent his body or soul from being strengthened. This is very common characteristic of prophets, for example, Manes, Jesus, Buddha and Mohammed. A journey to a barren place, where there just a few men-less women left, ruled by a crippled king, who fished in a boat, but he was able to overtake the hero reaching the castle of the Grail first and almost be his host... Does it bring to mind the devastation of a faithless land ruled by a playful devil?

The paraphernalia of the bleeding sword, the chorus of young people, the shining Grail which almost blinded Perceval, the banquet, the question that was not asked, the drowsiness and the awakening to find nothing... Should we compare it to Manes' stay in India or Jesus' forty day test in the desert? (We could find similarities in the other prophets' lives, what we know of them.) The symbols that a sorcerer interpreted for Perceval, was a kind of recognition of the prophet's own destiny; and the same as all the tests to be passed seemed to communicate of the religious message.

Perceval, Galahad and Bors praying before the Grail. Out of the one hundred and fifty knights who attempted this quest, they alone achieved this sublime instant.

Similarities cannot be drawn when comparing endings. Manes was killed and cut into pieces, while Jesus ended up on the cross. The Grail legend was written for human beings who belonged to the Middle Ages, in need of heroes, though. Heroes had made a comeback in troubadours' poems and in writers' romances and novels. Some knights actually existed, and each country's history made them into legends, such as El Cid, Roland and many others. Then literature was to create many more that seemed real.

That is why the Grail was so fascinating. It had been built from the most suitable material and it was what people wanted to hear. If, in addition, it coincided with the great heresy of Catharism or with the knights of the Temple Order, it had an ideal, a chimaera to stand up to the enemies of the Faith.

The Grail unquestionably came from Britain or England. In the Pyrenees the name 'grasal' was also given to a stone cup. The word could have undergone a change as Wolfram von Eschenbach wrote its legend, in the cycle corresponding to *Perceval*. He also confessed that he had heard it said by a certain Kyot the Provençal and it had appeared in Provence, which was swarming with Cathars in those times.

The legend's progress

We will let Gérard de Sède take us by the hand and lead us with a text taken from his passionate work *The Accursed Treasure:*

Relations between the British Isles and the Pyrenees region dated back to protohistory and were frequent under the reign of the Angevin dynasty of the Plantagenets. We know that by the beginning of the eighth century Arthurian legend had already been heard of in Spain, Portugal and Italy and that a bard called Bleddhri showed his talent as a narrator at the court of the troubadour prince Guillaume of Poitiers.

A little later, the author Huon of Bordeaux offered us extraordinary images of the meeting between the oldest Celtic traditions and the countries of Oc while Huon, a knight from Aquitaine, flouting a ban imposed by the Church, became friends with the dwarf Oberon, who was known as 'the little magic king'. He gave Huon the ring and the cup, which were going to allow him, on reaching the Country of Foix, to conquer Esclarmonde, and take her to the castle of Montmar. It is not surprising that the Grail legend contained so many British and southern elements, on account of the fact that their roots were developed in these territories.

As far as these territories are concerned, much is to be learned from the work by Wolfram. We will firstly point out, according to the old chronicler of Oc, Raimond d'Aguiliers, that it was the Count of Toulouse, Raimond of Saint-Gilles, who found the Holy Lance. He did so during a crusade in the siege of Antioch in 1098, acting under orders of an inexperienced monk, Barthélemy, who said he had been inspired by Saint Andrew. The Lance was later to be associated with the Christianised Grail. When commenting on this tradition Paul Alphandéry wrote:

To the extent that Welsh influence did not predominate the messianic hero, Raimond of Saint-Gilles was the prototype of the Grail kings; as for Kyot, he was the conveyor of the legend of Raimond.

Other factors point to the Oc country being present in the mind of the Grail poets, or at least of those, who like Wolfram, were contemporaries of the Albigensian crusade the 'Terre Gaste' which, barren due to a traitorous blow, could symbolize the Oc country in a poet's pen after being devastated; Perceval or Perzival also, stripped of his inheritance by his enemies, is the figure of the perfect Cathar. And finally, the name of Montsalvage, given by Wolfram to the Grail castle is unquestionably a name from the Oc country.

Having had their appetite opened by these resonances, some modern authors have gone further; tracking the Quest, the idea occurred to them to locate 'the dangerous castle' and determine the name of the hero who managed to dominate it...

The Cabalist message

In the end the Grail married infinite meanings and values. To Wolfram it was capable of giving longevity to the holder and spiritual fulfilment, like an initiation transformation. This is how cabalistic elements were introduced around the mythical object, or the treasure that so many men and women longed after.

It is worth bearing in mind that in the eleventh Century Cabala and all the thought that surrounded it were very present. There was a school in Moorish Toledo that studied it. Some historians take Kyot to this place, where he first discovered the Grail. Yet there were also other similar schools in Gerona, Montpellier and different parts of Europe. We should also not be surprised that one was founded in Troyes in 1070 and run by Rashi, who was probably one of the most famous Cabalists of the time.

As we all know, Cabala can be put on a level with a form of esoteric Judaism as it provoked a dramatic transformation in outlook. This aspect can also be found in different oriental religions such as Hinduism and Buddhism etc. Anybody that wanted to join the world of Cabala had to undergo an initiation process that would bring about a change in his outlook and then in his judgement. Given over to this permanent transformation, a moment would arrive when he could step outside of his body, a sort of re-incarnation or 'tiferet'. This process recalls the Perfect Cathars and their state of sublimation after achieving 'impeccability', that is, being beyond the possibility of sinning. It also brings to mind the reincarnation that they preached.

The Cabalists associated the 'tiferet' with a wise old man, an inscrutable king, a young hero, a sacrificed divinity, a curse, a bucket and a rosy cross. Almost all these elements are unquestionably found in the legend of the Grail.

Chapter VII
THE VIRTUES OF THE GRAIL

Forms of the Grail

In the different writings the Grail was represented in three forms:

1. Its nature was a complete mystery; for instance, we are told that it was *not made of wood, or of a known metal, stone, horn or bone*. An immaterial characteristic is that it has an activity of its own.

2. It was like a stone, which could be 'celestial' or 'bright'.

3. A receptacle, which may have been a cup or a vessel, made of gold and, on occasions, inlaid with precious stones. In this form, women always carried the chalice, which is contrary to the Christian tradition, in which it was carried by males in their status of priests.

There was another form that may be considered as being mixed on account of the Grail being formed inside a giant emerald.

This mythical object could be described as either 'holy' or 'rich'. In the novel *Le Morte d' Arthur* the following is written: *it is the richest thing that living people can possess.*

A supernatural light

The Grail almost always gave off a supernatural light that was not only blinding but also fascinating to such an extent that if somebody looked at it he lost all sense of reality. Robert de Boron in his work *Joseph of Arimathea* described the Grail as a great luminosity that preceded the Holy Spirit, the forty-two years that Joseph of Arimathea spent in prison seemed like three days to him as he enjoyed them in divine pleasure. To Wolfram von Eschenbach it was 'the stone of light'.

Chalice of Ardagh (Ireland) from the thirteenth century. Could the Grail have been like this one?

The perfect satisfaction of any desire, and paradise. The stone of light that no earthly brightness even came close to.

In the *Queste du Graal,* when Galahad contemplated the Grail he was overcome by an uncontrollable trembling, which prompted him to whisper:

Now I see clearly all that the tongue could never express, nor the heart think. Here is the beginning of the great boldness and the cause of the feats. Before me I have the marvel of all marvels.

In *Le Morte d' Arthur,* when the Grail appeared there was a roar of thunder, accompanied by *a flash a light seven times brighter than daylight.* At that moment, in that instant, everyone was illuminated by the grace of the Holy Spirit.

The food that nourished heroes

Wolfram says that the Grail nourished the Templars, because it mysteriously reached their table; then, each one of them took what he needed without anyone being left short, even though the divine vessel appeared only to contain food enough for one person.

Yet the food that the Grail provided was material, although it satisfied hunger, a physical feeling. It acted instead on the mind, making the person forget their need to eat but did not cease to nourish, so the privileged did not lose their strength and kept their youth. In *Perceval li Gallois* for instance, the guests at the table forgot to eat on simply smelling the aroma that the Grail gave off.

In the *Queste du Graal,* the divine vessel appeared when the knights were about to eat. Once it had given each his helping it suddenly disappeared, in the same way that it had appeared. Robert de Boron simplified the matter by writing: *It is called the Grail because it pleases the heroes.*

However, nobody fed off the Grail so much as Joseph of Arimathea in the forty-two years that he was King Crudel's prisoner. Every morning he took a host from the celestial vessel that quenched his hunger and thirst.

It granted life to the dying

The Grail could heal the dying and extend life in a supernatural way. In the novel by Manessier, Perceval and Hector fought for several days until they collapsed to the ground fatally wounded. They believed the end was near, and therefore reconciled by acknowledging that the other was the winner when neither of them could claim the victory for himself. That very night, an angel appeared carrying the Grail and healed them instantly.

A very similar sequence is found in *Le Morte d'Arthur,* when Lancelot is healed of his wounds. In the "Queste du Graal" a knight, left for dead on a bed, managed to drag himself along the ground over to where the Grail was. By merely touching it he recovered completely. The absence of wounds and physical exhaustion allowed him to devote himself to a dream full of promises.

The Grail was also capable of subjecting a king or a hero to a sort of lethargic death. This is how Wolfram explained it: *The Phoenix Bird burnt himself to ashes, but he did it to immediately reappear more beautiful than ever in all his splendour.*

There was clearly a relationship between the Grail as a source of life and regeneration; the Phoenix Bird has always epitomised regeneration. As we can see, the divine object could illuminate, feed and heal, yet none of the benefits could be granted to those who *were sullied with guilt on account of vile lies*. The trophy belonged to the pure, to those that had not known sin, not even an insinuation of it. Some lost this right for having loved a woman too much.

It provided victory and dominance

To Robert de Boron, all the fortunate ones that managed to contemplate the Grail would never lose whatever they possessed, be done justice in all disputes, win contests and maintain their dominance for a long time, being able to extend it if they so wished.

Wolfram von Eschenbach in *Parzival* wrote about somebody who passed the Grail test: *From that moment there will be nobody in the world with an edge on you in nobility or honour. You will be Lord of all creation. The supreme power has been transferred to you.*

As for dominance, the Grail was related to the sacred sword as it had obtained the celestial strength of royalty. It possessed supreme help, which made a hero invincible, as long as his intentions were noble and when dominating a new people he had to think more about his subjects' benefit than his own.

Its destructive power

The Grail did afford a destructive power, capable of blinding and killing. On occasions it became a whirlwind that flattened everything. When the evil Nescien discovered this divine object, he recognised that it was his most cherished dream; however, on opening it, he was blinded by its brightness and he fell convulsed to the ground and died.

In the *Queste du Graal,* we are told that Mordrain suffered a similar punishment for *daring to contemplate what no tongue can express.* It was a supernatural wind that harmed him, though, and his blindness could be healed if a hero capable of discovering the mystery of the Grail appeared.

In the Gerbert's novel, *Mondrain,* not to be confused with the previous character, managed to build an altar for the Grail. When he tried to visit it, though, he found the way blocked by an angel wielding a blazing sword, who told him that he could never die even if his injuries remained open and that he would have to wait for a knight to appear that really had gained the right to stand before the Grail. The work *Diu Crône* states that merely crossing the Grail is a fatal risk to take.

The ever-fearsome Siège Perilous

The Siège Perilous, the one that was empty at the Round Table, was fearsome for any undeserving person that tried to occupy it. An abysm could open up under his feet or he could be struck down by lightening. When Moses tried to sit on it he was snatched by seven hands of fire that *burnt him like a flame that destroyed a piece of resinous wood.* The text is even more mysterious because half the fire that consumed the victim could be put out while the other half remained alight until Galahad appeared, who was willing to undertake the great Grail adventure.

The Siège Perilous of the Round Table. French miniature from the fifteenth century.

The incident that took place at Joseph of Arimathea's table could be considered to be a variant, with all those sullied with guilt being drawn into an abysm that opened under their feet. This showed that apostles or knights that had lost their honour were impostors.

Who could search for the Grail?

Only those knights that had sat in a particular gold armchair made by a supernatural lady could search for the Grail. But six that attempted it were dragged through a sudden windstorm. When Parsifal sat down, a remarkable roll of thunder was heard, but he remained unperturbed. Then he was harassed by a multitude of extravagant people and faced them without moving, confident that nothing could move him because he was the bearer of the strength provided by his honour and his just behaviour.

To Robert de Boron, all the heroes that underwent this test, members of the Round Table for the most part, were ready to succeed in their quest. In *Le Morte d'Arthur,* the question is offered more openly: the Siège Perilous could only be occupied by those who had managed to overcome the sword challenge. This challenge consisted of drawing a sword out of a stone it was wedged into, just as King Arthur had done when he proved he was better than all the other knights.

At that moment of triumph, the Grail appeared in the victor's court, shining more brightly than the sun. It appeared magically to feed any knight in need of nourishment with its aroma.

Le Morte d'Arthur depicts Lancelot being drawn to a door by the immense brightness it gave off. He was under the impression that all the torches in the world had been lit. Suddenly a voice recommended he flee instantly, otherwise he would be destroyed, but the hero took no notice and entered. He was subject to terrible flames that brought him to the ground, where he remained motionless, having lost all strength in his limbs... Maybe he had gone too far, unaware that the sin of adultery weighed down on him?

His friends, on finding him in this state, believed him to be dead, but curiously an old one said: *In the name of God, he could never have died as now he is fuller of life than any of you.*

Lancelot remained in this situation for some twenty-four days. Then he woke up, without showing signs of being hungry or thirsty and surprised everyone by remarking: *Why have you pulled me out of that dream? I could never feel better.*

In effect, he had dreamt about the best aspect of the Grail: Paradise. He had been initiated into a new order, that of the Grail heroes, who would suffer any of the array of human weaknesses. However, he would never be able to see it.

When the Grail is made of stone

The stone Grail usually appears as sculpted from a material that dropped out of the sky. Wolfram von Eschenbach bestowed some powers on it that were quite similar to those of the alchemist elixir of regeneration. However, it does have the novelty of being brought to Earth by a chorus of angels that were condemned for having remained neutral during Lucifer's rebellion. Despite their being responsible for guarding the Grail, this never lost any of its virtues.

In time, the overseeing of the divine stone was bestowed upon some knights who were all carefully chosen by Heaven through a characteristic signal. According to the story, a stone fell from Lucifer's crown when it was struck by the Archangel Michael. And it became the stone of the Chosen, especially when it fell into the world of the mortals. Perceval received it from the hands of Titurel as he was the fortunate person to find it. Titurel became head of the dynasty of the Grail.

According to the legend, the fallen stone was an emerald that a faithful angel cut into the shape of a cup. Incidentally, the first to receive the cup was Adam while he was in Paradise. Once he was expelled from there, he lost it. However his son Set was able to locate it and he kept it until his death.

There is also another story that tells us that the Grail was hidden in the Pyrenees, close to Montségur, the sacred Catharian temple. The temple was the Cathars' ploy to evade Lucifer, who did not stop looking for it with all his court of demons. In a cave, perhaps at the bottom of a lake, was where it could be found. Otto Rahn believed this so strongly that he won Hitler and the Nazis over to his way of thinking. The intention was to unite the divine vessel to Longinus' Lance, part of the Hapsburgs' Viennese treasure. The belief was that with these two elements it would be easier to conquer the world. This was the Third Reich's dream on seeing how rapidly it had won control of half of Europe, while at the same time it filled almost all the nations of the five continents with fear.

An enlightening passage

So far we have discussed the virtues of the Grail along with other secondary subjects. We believe that the time has come to describe one of the key moments: the triumph of finding the Grail. For this we are going to take an enlightening passage from the book *The Quest for the Grail:*

...They heard a voice say, Whoever has not participated in the Quest for the Holy Grail must leave as he has no right to remain any longer.

No sooner had these words been uttered than King Pelles than his son Eliezer and the maiden left. When the room was empty, just with another two participants in the Quest, a man appeared to descend from the sky, dressed in similar fashion to a bishop, holding a cross and with a mitre on his head. Four angels were carrying him on a very elaborate chair and then they set him down next to the table on which stood the Holy Grail. The one who had been brought that looked like a bishop had letters on his forehead that said: Here is Josephes, the first bishop of Christendom, the same that Our Lord ordained in the city of Sarras, in the spiritual palace. *The knights saw this. Knowing about the letters, they found it very strange, as the Josephes the letters referred to had died more than three hundred years earlier. He spoke to them saying:*

Ah! Knights of God, servants of Jesus Christ do not be astounded if you see me before you as I am with this holy cup; the same way I served it on Earth, I am also its servant in spirit.

After saying this, he went over to the silver table, knelt down before the altar and leant on his elbows. After having been there for a long while he paid attention and heard the door to the room opening and slamming shut. He looked in that direction and the others followed suit: they saw the angels that had brought him leave, two of them carrying a candle each, the third a cloth of gold threaded red silk and the fourth, a spear that was bleeding abundantly and the drops falling into a bowl he was carrying in the other hand. They placed the two candles on the table. The third put the cloth next to the Holy Cup and the fourth held the lance completely straight over the bowl, in such a way that the blood that ran down the shaft dropped into it. As soon as this had been done, Josephes got up and withdrew the lance from over the Holy Cup to cover it with the cloth.

Subsequently, he looked as if he was going to perform the sacrament of mass. After remaining there for a short time, he took a wafer that had been made in the form of bread from the Holy Cup. On raising it, a child-like figure descended from the sky whose face was so red it burnt like fire: he went into the bread, in such a way that those that were in the room easily

saw that the bread was shaped like a man of flesh. After hold-
ing it up for a good while, Josephes put it back into the Holy
Cup.

After having done what a priest does during a service of
mass, he approached Galaz, he kissed him and told him to kiss
his brothers, which e did before telling them:

Servants of Jesus Christ, you have endeavoured and suffered
to see some of the marvels of the Holy Grail, sit at this table:
you will eat heartily the best food a knight has ever tasted,
shared out by the hand of our Saviour. You endeavoured at the
right time as it is today that you will receive the highest reward
a knight has ever received.

After saying this, Josephes disappeared from among them in
such a way that they did not know what had become of him.
They sat at the table with great sadness and began to cry with
such bitterness that their faces were left wet.

The companions then looked and saw a naked man rise out
of the Holy Vessel, with his hands, feet and heart bleeding, and
he said to them: Knights and servants of mine and of my loyal
son, in mortal life you have become spiritual, you have searched
so hard for me that I can no longer hide myself from you. You
need to see some of my secrets and mysteries, as you have done
so many things you are seated at my table where no knight has
eaten since the times of Joseph of Arimathea. The rest have had
what the servants have; that is, present-day knights and many
others have been satiated with the grace of the Holy Cup,
though they were never in the position that you are now. Take
and receive the high food that you have desired for so long and
worked so hard for.

So he took the Holy Cup himself and approached Galaz,
who knelt down when his Saviour gave it to him. He received
it willingly with clasped hands and each of the others did the
same, and nobody thought to refuse the bread-like piece he
put into their mouth. When they had all received the high food
that tasted so sweet and marvellous to them it was as if all the
delicacies that the heart could think of were inside their body.
The one that had satiated them in this way said to Galaz:

Son, as clean and pure as an earthly man can be, do you
know what I have in my hands?

Not at all, *he answered*. Not if you do not tell me.

It is, *he said* the bowl that Jesus Christ ate lamb from at the Passover supper with his disciples. It is the bowl that all those who I have found in my service have used; it is the bowl that no man of little faith saw without it weighing heavily on him. And because it has served all abundantly it must be called the Holy Grail. You have now seen what you wanted and desired so much, but you have not yet seen it uncovered as you will see it. Do you know where this will take place? In the city of Sarras, in the spiritual palace: that is why you will go from here in the company of this Holy Vessel. It will not be seen again and there will be no more strange happenings. Do you know why it is going? Because it is not used and honoured by those on the Earth as it should be. People who were satiated in the past by the grace of the Holy Vessel have reverted to a more impure and mundane life. And as they have repaid it so badly, I will strip them of the honours I granted them. That is why tomorrow morning you shall go to the sea and find the ship where you took the Sword of the Strange Tahali; so you do not go alone, I want you to take Perceval and Bors with you. I do not wish you to leave this land until the Crippled King has been healed; you shall take blood from this lance and you shall smear it on his legs; this way he will be healed as nothing else can cure him.

A brief reflection

As we can see, the triumph of seeing and enjoying the Grail was accompanied by the presence of Jesus Christ. Despite the fact that in the end it leaves behind a trace of sadness, the impression is so intense that Galaz will go through the stages that death holds for him: the destiny warranted by a saintly hero. This was an ending that the Roman Church of the time would expect, yet it still refused to recognise this work, like the others, which are all worthy of being recommended to the faithful as compulsory reading.

Chapter VIII

THE THUNDERBOLT, THE LANCE
AND VENGEANCE

Meteorite stones

It is impossible to know when the legends started claiming as their own the stones that fall from the sky, which were confused, on many occasions, with the ray of lightning that appears in a cloudless sky. They are small meteorites that primitive human beings thought of as magical, on account of their exceptional nature.

R. Guénon identified the myth of the meteorite stones with flint axes; when first used to kill, they were seen as the ray of lightning that splits and destroys. That is why they ended up in the mythologies of different countries. We have found a connection between the axes and Siva or Thor as they were used as hammers to strike down warriors that emerged from the bowels of the Earth.

The stone axe was also transformed into the bolt of lightning of the Olympian divinity Zeus, who used it to exterminate the Titans. However, in the hands of Indra, the god and celestial warrior of the Indo-Aryan tribes, it became Vajra, in other words, a sceptre, a thunderbolt and an immaculately pure stone.

The Irish saga of Peronnik is relatively similar to the Grail legend. It varies in that a gold jug and a diamond-studded spear were used to effectively conquer the castle of the giants. The jug's powers are as follows:

It immediately produces food and necessary riches on request. If drunk from, injuries are healed, illnesses are cured regardless of how acute they may be and the dead are resuscitated, provided that the beneficiaries are carriers of the most absolute purity and promise never to sin.

Yet the diamond spear had no mercy, it acted inexorably. It was as bright as a lively flame. If a noble hero held it, victory would be his. That is why when Peronnik was wielding it, the earth started to tremble, a deafening roll of thunder was heard, the palace, where he was enclosed, disappeared, and he found himself in a wood with a spear and a gold jug; two magic objects that he could take to the king of Britain.

Angels may have been bearers of the Grail, which was received by the purest and most heroic knight.

Paradise in relation to the Grail

Many authors associated the Grail with Paradise. Wolfram von Eschenbach considered it to be *such a sublime object that Paradise does not contain anything more beautiful: the flower*

*of all happiness brings such an abundance of graces to Earth
that its virtues are equal to those attributed to the Kingdom of
Heaven.*

In the *Queste du Graal,* when Galahad saw the Grail in the
spiritual palace he was overcome by a series of marvellous shiv-
ers, compelling him to implore God to take him far away from
this life to enter Paradise as he could not be wiser having known
the Secret of the Grail.

In *Perceval li Gallois,* the Grail castle is given the name
Eden, whereas in the *Diu Crône,* Galvano, in his continual quest
for the Grail, reached a country *that looked to him like Paradise
on Earth.* We have already mentioned that Set found the Grail,
and he found it precisely where Paradise had been, where his
parents had been expelled from.

The dual power of the lance and the cup

In the range of symbols used by the different Grail traditions,
the lance can be seen as the 'axis of the world'. This weapon
also unites the meanings of 'regal' and 'polar'. By using it as a
literary element it clearly performs two functions: it injures and
it heals. This is not necessarily a contradiction as it can be
explained.

The lance often appears bleeding, doing so to such an extent
that this liquid flows along the blade. In the *Diu Crône,* the king
used the blood as food. In later texts the vital liquid of human
beings acquired greater importance, overshadowing the object
that contained it. It has also been called *Sangreal*, with the claim
that it represents the blood of Jesus Christ and of the king simultaneously. Christians logically chose the first version over the
second and connect it to the lance that injured their Master in the
side while he was on the cross. They therefore considered the
blood to be *of redemption*, that is, a regenerating element.

However, the lance was capable of injuring Nescien when he
was trying to learn about the Grail; it left him blind and dying.
He could only save himself when blood sprang from the shaft of
the lance. Something similar occurred in the 'Grand St. Graal,
although in this instant an angel appeared and heralded the mar-

vels that were to occur in each of the counties that Joseph Arimathea visited.

The reason for such extravagances was so that in the course of the adventures *true knights were to be distinguished from impostors, the earthly knights were to become celestial, repeating the miracle of the blood that sprang from the shaft of the lance.*

Furthermore, the last king of the dynasty of Joseph was to be injured in both thighs by the lance. These injuries could not be healed until a fortunate knight appeared who was capable of discovering the Grail secret as he possessed the moral and spiritual standing needed to succeed in such a venture. This allows us to deduce that the lance was associated with the character of the heroic 'restorer'.

Was vengeance necessary?

In many Grail texts, a vision of necessary vengeance is given. The predestined hero had to conform to this vision to succeed. For instance, when the shaft of the spear was taken out of a knight's dead body, responsibility for revenge was assumed. Whoever received this mission was usually also obliged to discover the Grail mystery.

Peredur, a sort of Perceval or Perzival, is a hero of a Celtic legend. He was cursed for not having been capable of *asking the question about such an extraordinary sized spear that sprang three drops of blood before his eyes.* He did not do it because he was astounded by the shining Holy Grail, along with all the paraphernalia that took place in the main room in the Castle of the old, grey-haired king, who was a replica of the Fisher King. He promised the following:

On my honour, I will never sleep with peace of mind until I manage to discover the story of this magic spear.

The legend concluded as Peredur exterminated the women warriors of Kaerlay who possessed supernatural powers. He got his revenge through them as they had dared to kill the king's son, and at the same time, they harmed him leaving him a grey-haired, defenceless cripple. Through vengeance, the king recovered his strength and furthermore, the region regained its prosperity.

It is of interest that these supernatural women realised that *Peredur was well trained to defeat them because he had learnt chivalry in a school close to where they lived.* This clearly shows that a human being is capable of overcoming all powers, even supernatural ones. He must however be moved by a supreme spiritual force, which can only be given by faith in the form of a glorious destiny. The same occurs in the religions that reward their followers with Paradise.

The poisoned lance

The fundamental themes of the old Celtic legend of Peredur coincide perfectly with those of the saga of Parsifal and, at the same time, with some traditions far removed from Christianity. In many of these texts a lance appears and is accompanied by a receptacle containing poisoned blood with permanent flames coming out, which enhances its deadly appearance.

Symbolic image of the quest for the Grail that was imposed on all the Knights of the Round Table, but only a few were to successfully rise to the challenge.

The shaft of the lance, which was plunged into the blood, extinguished the flames, but it was reinforced with a deadly power. Due to this property, when Amfortas, the Fisher King, was injured with the lance, he knew he could never be healed and above all, if he stayed alive it was because everything around him had died or lacked the vitality it needed to recover from physical or moral ruin, That is why the lament was formulated: *God has subjected me to the worst of his powers.*

We already know that in the end he was healed, and at the same time prosperity returned to his kingdom, thanks to the intervention of the hero Perceval.

The dolorous blow

In the *Queste du Graal,* the Fisher King was wounded several times whilst fighting against King Crudel, an enemy of the Christians. But these wounds were not mentioned until he went blind due to getting too close to the Grail. This can be thought of as the dolorous blow because the human being that suffered it recognized his weaknesses. Together with his awkward soberness, he understood that he had aimed to attain something that was superior to his strength or which he still did not deserve. That is why he lost all notion of everything that did not fall inside his limits. His blindness was necessary to focus his mind on nothing but his own mistake of having aimed too high.

The dolorous blow could be related to a recumbent sword like the one that was found close to the gold crown on Solomon's vessel. This sword was accompanied by a scabbard which has the phrase 'memory of blood' engraved on it. In the *Morte d'Arthur,* this weapon had been carved partly with the wood of the 'Tree of Life' because it was awaiting the hero that could handle it, the only one who could do so. When Nescien wielded it in his fight against a giant, the tough blade ended up broken. However, Mordrain was able to repair it, which does not mean that Nescien could not be harmed by the red-hot sword, brandished by a merciless invisible hand.

Pelles met a similar fate when he tried to draw the magic sword. He received the dolorous blow of a lance in the thigh. He was not to be healed of his injury until Galahad, the one who was predestined to discover the Grail secret, appeared.

In the *Morte d' Arthur,* one of the leading characters was Sir Balin le Savage and he was given the name of the 'Knight with the Two Swords' as with them he could deal fatal blows, similar to King Arthur's Excalibur.

The broken sword

In *Gautier de Doulens* we find Galvano. He was responsible for avenging a knight whose dead body had retained part of his sword Galvano had tried to pull out. This did not seem to frighten him as he kept part of the blade. He went to the Grail castle taking the dead body in a coffin and upon reaching the surroundings of the drawbridge, he met the king who was naturally surprised by the fact the man was carrying a broken sword, the other part of which seemed to be stuck in the body inside the coffin.

It occurred to him to ask Galvano to put the two pieces together, something the hero could not do as he did not have sufficient power. The king acknowledged this by saying that he still had to pass some tests before daring to contemplate the Grail, which would allow him, together with other prodigies, to put the sword back together. The king immediately informed Galvano about the situation in the region: the blow had impoverished the kingdom of Logres and its monarch, as we have seen, was gravely injured.

Galvano fell asleep, though, because he was not ready to listen to a story that could lead him to discover the Grail mystery. The knight's powerlessness had been clearly demonstrated, at least, to the king, after seeing that he had not been able to put the two pieces of sword back together. If he had managed to do so, he would have gained the power to restore health and wealth to the kingdom of Logres.

When Galvano passed the necessary tests, he would be able to repair the sword. Listening to the king's story and not falling asleep in the presence of the gleaming Holy Grail would allow him to ask the key question, or 'pose the question' that would bring about the happiest ending — the healing of the king and the resurrection of the whole of Logres.

Why was Logres punished?

When King Amagon decided to stand up to the 'Women of the Fountain', he did not hesitate in taking one of his fiercest knights with him to be at his side. This helped him to get his hands on a gold cup, after wreaking havoc in a peaceful land. However, everything changed in the face of a desire for revenge, until its female overlords subjected Logres to a curse: ruin was to befall it in all its senses, while the king was to become an old cripple. Oddly enough, this monarch was the master of the Grail castle and its throne remained unoccupied for a thousand bitter years.

Arthur had to be crowned for Galvano to later find out about what had happened. He rode to Logres where he arrived in the company of a knight's corpse and a broken sword. In the novel *Perceval,* Wolfram also portrayed Klinscher as another assailant of women, but in this case it was adultery, not theft of a gold cup combined with assault, which led to the same outcome.

Klinscher possessed a mysterious castle where he managed to attract women by bewitching them. One of his victims was Arthur's mother. Galvano reached there and ended up rescuing Orgeluse, the woman that had brought ruin to the Grail castle and the Fisher King.

Parsifal

In the novel *Gerbert de Montreuil,* Parsifal also assumed responsibility for avenging Gurnemant, the master that taught him to use weapons together with the arts of chivalry, after extracting the sword that had caused death from him. Later, when he arrived at King Arthur's court, he contemplated the surprising scene of a boat, navigated by a swan, with a coffin on its circular roof that nobody could open.

Only Parsifal managed it. He also discovered that he would have to take revenge for this man's body too. However, the man suddenly woke up and took him by the neck to put him inside the coffin. The next thing he did was to run to Parsifal's saddle. Parsifal managed to escape from the coffin and immediately freed himself of such a dangerous enemy, as it was the devil himself. After passing the tough test, the hero rode to the castle of the Grail where he was able to put the sword back together that had broken previously while he was fighting.

'Apparent death'

The symbolism of the swan, the coffin and the 'not-dead' body are important to bear in mind because in many texts on the Holy Grail we find 'apparent women': they are human beings with special properties. They lived in their own kingdom, which was veiled in a sort of lethargic physical and spiritual mystery. Yet there was a shred of hope, provided by the chosen one in his attempt to discover the mystery contained within the divine recipient.

A beautiful lady usually accompanied the knights who failed. She was also related to the hero, whom she supplied with valuable information.

101

In the *Diu Crône,* when Galvano posed the key question before the Holy Grail, the Fisher King shrieked with joy and then offered this explanation: the entire kingdom had been dead for a long time, although some of its occupants seemed alive because of the anxiety of thinking that nobody could ever bring the quest for the Holy Grail to a close consumed them.

Strangely, when the Fisher King handed the sword to Galvano, which would make him become an ever-triumphant hero, everything disappeared — the monarch who had just been healed, the castle and above all, the Holy Grail. This should be interpreted as the kingdom being re-established, but somewhere other than where they had suffered so much misfortune.

In *Perceval,* the restoration occurred in a different way. The hero discovered the Grail mystery and then sat on a throne that had belonged to the Fisher King. The following novelty was also introduced: in the castle was to be found Titurel, a bed-ridden old man and he was the first person in charge of defending the Holy Grail. Materially, he was dead but he could not 'die in peace' until the predestined hero appeared, though he took four hundred or a thousand years to do so.

The knights that failed

In the Grail text none of the human beings, objects or situations, are used gratuitously. Each one is a symbol. For example, when the hero found a dead knight, there was often a lady beside him. This should be interpreted as somebody that had failed in his quest for the Holy Grail. However, when a newcomer collected his sword, the corpse became a motive for vengeance, his death would then not have been in vain as it would have served as a stimulus or compromise for whoever was to triumph in the most sublime venture.

On the other hand, the woman found with the corpse was usually related to the hero, the benefit being that he would inform her of his true name and, in addition, give her important information about his origins and she would often reproach him on account of his not having *asked the question* or *posed the key question*. This means she had divine powers as we assume she was not present in the room of the Castle when the dazzling Holy Grail appeared.

Of course she could have heard that a knight, a relation of hers, had entered the castle to discover the Grail mystery. When the awaited miracle of *annulling all misfortune* did not occur, it was easy for her to understand what had happened. She must have been expecting something of this sort to happen. The knight lying down dead next to her was also pursuing the objective of being the first to find the divine recipient: but he was faced by a stronger enemy that took his life.

The woman that found Parsifal was Sigune, and she cursed him for having been indifferent before the presence of the sacred weapons, a sword and a spear, and the Holy Grail. On that occasion, the damage did not only affect the kingdom but it also reached King Arthur's court, which lost its past splendour and, at the time, was subject to continuous wars that spread over the entire face of the earth.

When Parsifal arrived at the Grail castle, the Fisher King had died and Chastel Mortel was on the throne. As the hero had obtained three sacred objects, he forced his enemy to take his own life. He was not concerned if there was a new king in that region, though, as he went somewhere else, together with his accompanying knights, to where the Grail was to appear again, as a divine voice had told him so. We do not know if this happened because the story comes to an end at that passage.

Chapter IX
THE GRAIL CASTLE

The 'fish of wisdom'

In Celtic legends, a 'fish of wisdom' is mentioned. It could burn the hands of whoever picked it up yet it granted the individual all its knowledge if it was placed directly in his or her mouth, after being fished from the river with a rod. It was said that when the main race in Ireland, represented by Portholan, became extinct, there was only one survivor Tuan, who changed into different animals without losing his memory.

In the times of Tuatha dé Danann, Tuan turned into an eagle or a sparrow hawk. But he became a fish when the Milhead race came to power. Since he was caught and eaten by a princess at this time, he recovered his human form inside her stomach. Once he had been born into normal existence he had to wait to puberty to exercise his mission as a prophet.

This legend could possibly be linked to the Fisher King, who in many texts also acted as a guardian of the Grail, especially insofar as reincarnation is concerned. If the truth be told, this character had his origin in Joseph of Arimathea, in the Christian tradition, and the multiplation of the fishes. The author Robert de Boron tells us anyone that called the holy cup by its real name was deserving of the title 'rich fisherman' as the Grail was linked to a sacred fish.

On the other hand, Moorish legends in the Middle Ages, which are very well known in Spain, talked of a fish together with a stone of power. This stone had been mounted onto a ring and was a diamond, emerald or ruby. It was said to belong to Solomon, who lost it in the sea, but found it in the stomach of a fish that he himself had caught. That is how he recovered his power over visible and invisible forces, whether human beings, animals or devils. One of the ring's properties was *fire that could invade Heaven and Earth*. This invited it to be sought after with the same enthusiasm that the Knights of the Round Table and others from the island of Britain devoted to the Grail.

When the hero reached the surroundings of the Grail castle he knew his armour and weapons would be of no use to him.

The symbolism of the fish

It is very difficult, if not impossible, to locate the origins of the great legends, especially when they are used as regal or religious symbols. For instance, Alexander the Great was also said to have found a ring inside a gigantic fish he himself had freshly fished out of the Mediterranean. This jewel or stone was original in that it shone in the night like a powerful light, which is similar to what occurs with the Holy Grail.

To Christians, fish are a reminder of the words that Jesus Christ said to his apostles: *I want to make you fishermen of men.* Peter then assumed the role of 'foundation stone of the Church' at his Master's will. These are two very important factors when looking at the Fisher King and fish. Chrétien de Troyes tells us that only thing the king of the Grail could do was fish as he was so badly injured that he had to remain seated most of the time.

In *Perceval li Gallois,* the Fisher King used a gold hook. While he was on the river bank, he pointed out the way to the Grail castle to the awaited hero. He then appeared there as a sick king. Earlier he had confessed in his own words *everything he fished from the river did not cover his needs.*

The home of the Grail

A castle or an island could be home to the Grail, but it was never easily accessible, a kind of 'spiritual building' or a 'dwelling of souls'. This gives the idea that only the pure would enter, even if they were unaware or made the mistake of not asking the question at the right moment.

The castle was also portrayed as being invisible or out of reach. If the chosen reached it, it was on account of a spell or because it had appeared in an unexpected form. In "Perceval", the venture turned out to be impossible for the unchristened, as the *water allowed all beings we call creations to prosper. Our eyes see when we are spiritually bathed because souls acquire a brilliance that not even angels possess.*

The author of *Parzival* presents us with a chosen knight who arrived at the castle by a very unusual route. No sooner did he emerge from the woods than he took a route *that a bird would,* we are then led to imagine that the man and the animal flew off together. The author unquestionably represents our affective side in this way, as if the mere fact of wanting something sufficed to be able to have it. In this case, they wanted to move immediately from one place to another without having to walk or ride.

The castle could have been so impregnable that not even the most powerful armies were able to conquer it; on occasions, this place was called Montsalvatsche, *and there, if you advance it is not without facing a dangerous battle or you go in search of the atonement that everyone refers to as death.*

Wolfram von Eschenbach firmly supports the idea that the Templars defended the home of the Grail by preventing those knights from entering whose name was not written on the base of the divine recipient. Their devotion reached such extremes that they were capable of giving their last drop of blood to hold back an invader.

In other cases the castle was located on a hill which was impossible to locate without the guidance of a hero or angels. The Holy Grail appeared over the building supported by invisible hands. It was a wondrous sight, capable of converting anyone instantaneously; if the knight still harboured any doubt at that point in the quest, at that moment he realized he had gained the greatest of all victories.

An intentional modification

The first authors of poems and novels to write on this subject depicted the Grail as a well-fortified castle, never a church or religious temple of any description. However, in later texts an intentional modification appeared and the Grail was placed on an altar or in a chapel, which clearly refers to the Eucharist although it is not stated. The divine recipient was portrayed as a chalice used during mass, the one raised at the time of the Consecration.

Yet none of this appeared in Celtic legend, which gave shape to stories about the Grail. This leads us to assume this change was intentional. The aim would have been to introduce the Christian idea and it was later accepted in the belief that it enhanced the general storyline. Robert de Boron, in his work *Joseph of Arimathea* gave the Holy Grail a completely Christian identity, while continuing to use a wealth of esoteric elements.

An important point should be underlined here, and that is that religion is not symbolized by a simple conversion but by a whole complicated initiation process, which is very risky, lengthy and lonely, given that only a select group of privileged individuals were to succeed. A period of apprenticeship accompanied by pure sacrifice is almost that is required to reach the highest ranks of the church: the cardinalate or the papacy.

We should be heedful of the fact that Grail adventures constantly put lives in jeopardy; the perils to be overcome were often supernatural in character.

The resting place of the Grail is an initiation centre of a sort where the legacy of primordial tradition is maintained in accordance with the two most important dignities of the Middle Ages: the regal and the spiritual, or the Crown and the Church.

The most exciting adventure

Perceval contain the following conclusive statement: *Any knight who sets out to conquer the Holy Grail is forced to make his way to this sacred object with his weapons in hand.* In effect, we have before us a literature charged with the most exacerbated violence, betrayals of all kinds, noble gestures that reach the sublime, magic that pushed reality to the limits of madness, passions brimming with jealously or purity of two virginal beings, and all the rest of the broad universe that shaped the Grail adventures.

When Chrétien de Troyes wrote his poem on the Holy Grail, he based it on other previous works that specialists are learning about after very close analysis. Not satisfied with the idea of Celtic inspiration, some look to Greek mythology and traditions from India, the deserts of Persia as well as some countries in the Near East.

Seeds of emotion and bits and pieces of what most drew people's attention were brought together in this first work devoted to the Grail. It was the adventure that people wanted to read with all the essential elements to excite readers, both male and female, while making them feel they could experience it, albeit in a more serene way.

*In the quest for the Holy Grail, the knight had to reach a large
number of mysterious castles, guided on occasions by dogs emerging
rfrom deep inside the wood.*

The ensuing writers gradually modified the work as they
thought fit or as a result of the pressure of the people who were
paying them. Kings and nobles fulfilled the role of patron
through assuring the writers of a generous pecuniary assignation
and social standing, while at the same time offering them a com-
fortable workplace in their castle. This is why all the works
started off with a dedication to the lord who had 'financed'
them. It was standard practice for these patrons to read what was

written or to delegate this job to one of their most important advisers. When the original was approved, the order was given for copies to be produced, all of which were done by hand.

Thousands of symbols

The Grail stories can be read, quite simply, as a mere collection of adventures, which leave the sensation of having had a very exciting experience, or we can devote ourselves to studying the thousands of symbols contained in them. For instance, the main storyline is the quest for the divine receptacle, which can be construed as a *path of self-realization in which a holy war is unleashed against personal weaknesses or temptations*. To achieve it the knight needed to be a trained warrior with a 'number one' ranking, have extensive knowledge in all fields including occultism, and possess a solid vocation.

As far as vocation is concerned, Perceval and Parzival felt it when listening to the birds sing. They had surely heard these sounds before, but, it was at that exact moment they acted on it, as if the birds were messengers of God, angels or supernatural creations. These heroes were to leave immediately in search of adventure, although their mothers refused to allow them to go at the outset. They persevered tenaciously. Despite their mothers' foreboding about the immense danger that lay ahead for their sons, their resistance was worn down.

In Perceval's case his mother let him go, but on a scraggy and ailing horse. Furthermore, she did not give him suitable clothes. In the end, she died seeing her most loved one leave and he did not return to rescue her. Destiny, the realization of a vocation had become a need superior to any type of earthly love.

Leaving his mother to die was a contradictory start to the quest of the person who was to become the supreme representative of chivalry or nobility. Authors tried to correct that mistake later by making women or old men intervene to tell the hero that his mother died on seeing him leave, giving the idea that he was unaware of this.

An element that cancels out the mistake of his mother's death to a certain extent is the fact that the hero *lived in a time of ignorance*. From his arrival at Arthur's court, this ignorance would lead him to make decisions without consulting adults such as killing a knight who offended Queen Guinevere. On the other hand, he was to show his bravery and skill in handling a very primitive weapon, namely, the lancet. Later, after going through his master's or instructor's hands, he was in a 'pure state', ready to face the supreme feat of going off in search of the Holy Grail. He could no longer make mistakes, except for the ones that were owing to a sudden bout of astonishment such as having the Holy Grail before him for the first time, or a spell. A spell was to prevent him from repeating the experience, although he undertook a long string of adventures, and between each one he was to be reproached for his 'immense mistake'.

When inconsistency works

We are describing the beginning of the popular adventure novels, although the ones on the Grail contain a multitude of symbols and esoteric and religious messages. They are relatively similar to Homer's "The Odyssey" as far as the long journey is concerned. In the course of this voyage tragic events occur, which are obstacles to be overcome in order to attain the final goal, so deeply desired.

However, what the ingenious Greek writer left well resolved is not the case with Arthurian poems and novels. A close read would lead us to see that there are narrative loose strings and situations are not sufficiently explored and inconsistency is overused, something that works in this case because it is situated within the realm of the unreal. Once one goes further into the adventures, the excitement felt makes the reader become an accomplice to them, a kind of devotee, even the most absurd is admissible and reiterations accepted. There are episodes that are very similar to others already read; but they form part of the staircase, they are steps that lead to the floors where pleasures and thrills are waiting.

Adventure in its pure state

In the *Grand St. Graal*, we find Mordrain taken away by the Holy Spirit to a Tower-Island in the middle of the ocean. Once on solid ground, he was tempted by a woman, whom he rejected. Then, he discovered that she was Lucifer himself. But the perils were not over as he was at the mercy of a violent storm, with rolls of thunder that turned the brain, while bolts of lightening seemed to be aimed at him. When the atmosphere calmed down, a kind of phoenix swooped down and injured him seriously. He remained unconscious for seven days until he woke up in a nightmare, the interpretation of which allowed him to know the dynasty that would provide the hero who would discover the mystery of the Holy Grail.

A very similar adventure was experienced by Mordrain himself when a vessel reached the island carrying a coffin, a sword worthy of a hero and a gold crown, which was related to the 'Tree of Life'. The conquest of all these trophies involved a great effort and numerous perils.

In the *Queste du Graal,* Parsifal was surprised to find himself in front of a shining tree that changed into a chapel when he was just a few inches away from the trunk. Before the altar of the chapel lay the dead body of a knight. Suddenly, an invisible hand put out all the candles, which meant that hero could not escape from there. When he returned, he heard from the lips of a hermit that he could have been a victim of Lucifer, who had already killed a large number of brave knights and then buried them in the immediate surroundings of the tree.

The next morning, while Parsifal was sitting under a holm oak he saw a saddled horse arrive. No sooner had he mounted it though than he saw that it was a devilish creature and could not stop as it was galloping at the speed of a hurricane. This is how he ended up being thrown off into a stream of water but he managed to get out thanks to a mysterious boat. In it he discovered a woman that reminded him of his wife Blanchefleur. Finally, he reached an island where he found a lion about to be devoured by a gigantic snake. He managed to save the lion. A little later he resisted the evil provocations of a woman who was acting under a devilish influence. Then, a monk appeared driving a boat that Parsifal could use to get off the island and reach a castle where he was to face a test consisting of soldering the broken sword.

As can be seen from these incomplete storylines of the two novels on the Grail, the adventure is offered in its purest form: strange things continually happened, the hero was in constant battle and he kept escaping thanks to rather timely help that still seemed unexpected. However, this would not impress people at the end of the twentieth century surely, as they read and saw similar themes. However, if we imagine back to mid-way through the Middle Ages, literature was in its infancy and the adventures heard or written shocked, and even more so if they contained these elements.

The importance of the horse

In his splendid work *The Mystery of the Grail* Julius Evola tells us the following:

His horse could take the hero anywhere, even to mysterious castles where the most beautiful ladies were slaves to spells that had to be broken.

If the knight represented the spiritual beginning of the personality undergoing different tests, the horse shaped the one that 'bore the beginning', that is, the vital force that has been dominated. In the same way, in the classical myth referred to by Plato, the human personality is represented as a charioteer whose destiny is linked to his ability to dominate symbolic chargers.

In Antiquity, for two divinities the horse was sacred: Poseidon and Mars. The first was considered to be an earthly god ('earthquake'), at the same time the king of the sea, which is what made him the symbol of elemental force, and the second was linked to the warrior instinct, the 'vehicle', the horse, in the quest for the Holy Grail. When the hero was thrown off violently, he was defenceless as he lacked his best collaborator. We can see when 'the false dead body' managed to put Galvano in the coffin, he immediately ran to takeaway his horse because it would be the best way to defeat him. We know he was unsuccessful.

Even more mysterious literature

Anyone who is familiar with symbolic literature knows that storms and bolts of lightening, turbulent water, kidnappings, apparent deaths and similar happenings should be seen as being part of an initiation process. They are found in the *Tibetan Book of the Dead,* in the *Mitral Ritual* in esoteric Taoism, in Yoga and the cabalistic tradition of Merkaba.

One of the most remarkable adventures is that of the Castle of Marvels, when Cundrei, the extremely ugly messenger, said to Parzival: *The fights that you have faced until now were just child's play. Distressing events now await you.* She also made it her job to reproach him for not asking the key question before the Holy Grail. And continued in the same negative way: *Your forced apologies are insincere. Your reputation has proved to be impure. The Round Table has jeopardised its glory admitting Sir Perceval.*

From this moment, the hero is obliged to correct the mistake. One of his best collaborators was his horse as he is part of his person and, on occasions, even part of his spirit on account of the animal feeling part of the soul's emotions. That is why it runs at the sight of fire, presses on towards a haunted castle, and is never frightened in the face of the greatest horrors.

The definitive sword

The hero's first sword should be considered as the symbol of purely belligerent virtues, while the second is usually the definitive one. Parsifal obtained it in the Grail castle from the hands of Sigune, who says: *If you find out the secret virtues, you will be able to face any battle fearlessly.*

This sword could break, and to weld it so that it recovered all its powers without the repair being discovered, it had to be submerged in a Fountain. It meant the hero had overcome one of the last steps, the test that he was ready to 'raise the issue' or to ask the 'key question'. He may now know the essence of the Grail, uncover the mystery of the 'Stone of Light' or the 'Foundation Stone'.

The Fisher King will be resuscitated, or he will disappear to another life where eternal peace awaits him, and the entire kingdom will be prosperous again. Curiously, Parsifal was overcome by great nostalgia on finding out that the final moment had come:

The time may be near or far for me to be given the Grail again, until then I shall know no more enjoyment. It is the Grail that all my thoughts centre on. Nothing will take my mind off it while I am alive.

The transformation mentioned in the earliest texts has been brought about in the hero: *On finishing the sacred work, the supreme desire, we know that we are no longer the same, we have turned weakness into strength, heavy into light, material into spiritual.* In effect, Perceval, Parsival, Parsifal and the other knights that crown the subtle sublime venture are the 'Lords with the two Swords': he has taken possession of political power and the highest levels of spirituality.

Repairing the sword

In the third part of *Le conte du Graal* an anonymous writer introduced an interesting sequence:

He saw clearly that Perceval was carrying the sword at his waist that he had made himself and he knew very well that it was broken.

Vassal, *he said to him.* Due to a great sin you have broken the sword that I forged a long time ago. I can see that you broke it at the door of Paradise and you know that only I can repair it and I can only do it once. *So he opened the bolt and added* Vassal, come down and give me your sword and I will put the two pieces back together and there will be no danger of it breaking no matter how much you use it. This sword can only belong to a noble and brave man, no coward can possess it.

Perceval heard it and without any further hesitation he took out his sword and gave it to the man, who was certainly no fool, he roused the fire that never went out with a pair of big bellows. He took the two halves and put them together before forging the sword again so well that it did not look as if it had ever been broken. Then he polished the valuable sword and went over the letters that were written on it and finally he put it into the scabbard and said:

I tell you, vassal, that you will be named the best knight in the world. You have undergone many dangerous tests because of the Grail and you will still have many more winters and summers of tests. Now I can tell you that, knowing that I will not live much longer.

Once he had finished speaking he handed the sword to him and Perceval girded his sword and took his leave of him...

Chapter X
THE SUBLIME QUEST

Taking part is what counts

When reading all the texts on the Grail, one realizes that in the end it is almost irrelevant whether the quest ended in triumph or failure. From an emotional standpoint it is not understood in this way; however, on seeing the great effort that is needed just to gain the right to belong to the Round Table, the quantity of fatal adventures to be overcome on the way and the drain on the spirit and the person's physical condition, until reaching perfection, we must accept one truth: taking part is what counts.

This is what encourages the enormous accumulation of efforts, time and sentiments consumed. There is no other undertaking more difficult in the world, not even in the initiation into any religion or sect is the person required to pass such tests.

The first step in the quest for the Grail is 'action', but in a superlative degree. The hero must remain awake, keeping his reflexes alert and his sword ready. In the woods, on the steepest hillsides perils can appear. The danger lying ahead is rarely known, so the worst should be assumed.

Action is also required when coming upon the sweetest damsel with an injured bird or any other harmless object, as it could be a lure, a trap aiming to distract the hero's attention. This is a treacherous way of wearing him down while it was openly acknowledged to be impossible. A hero's reputation always goes before him. There were many who knew that fighting openly against him would lead to their death.

Getting to the bottom of the unknown

The unknown carries a warning that the instructor or master alerts the hero to. However, he will never talk about supernatural power, even if it comes in the form of a giant, several knights trying to fight against the chosen one at the same time or a seductive lady. What is announced is linked to witches, monsters and all supernatural powers that can cause shudders verging on terror. They will injure the deepest part of the conscience, until reaching the bounds of madness.

The hero may be skilful in handling weapons and horses but he will never cease to be a man plagued with doubts.

As authors sympathized with heroes, they started using a resource, as if they felt sympathy for the heroes, of the appearance of hermits or mysterious women, who would guide him at the most complicated moments or explain to him what had just happened. The basic aim was to allow them to eliminate the consequences of the terror provoked by some ghostly apparition.

Many historians draw a parallel between the tests in the quest and those of an apprentice shaman endeavouring to acquire real awareness of danger through his master's guidance. There are many similarities among the different versions of the quest for the Grail and the accounts of the shamans' ecstatic journeys. The symbolism is usually similar: the shaman aims to cure the ill and goes to look for their soul wherever it could have got to; he will fight against the demons of the Other Word and his definitive intervention will achieve regeneration just like the action of the Grail.

Links with alchemy should not be sought

Jean Markale in his magnificent book *Le cycle du Graal* tells us the following:

… It is difficult to claim that the Quest for the Grail is a description of alchemist operations of the Great Work. The truth is, many elements can be considered to be alchemic but it is doubtful that alchemist tradition was known in times as far back as the ones when the archetype of the quest was formed. The fact that in Peredur *and a little in Wolfram is where we find more references to the Art of Philosophers should put us on our guard. Alchemy has a clearly Mediterranean origin, and the archetype of the search is Celtic, probably Irish. That does not mean that the Irish clergies, transcribed at the same time texts from classical antiquity and of island traditions; because alchemy did not really start to gain importance before 1200 and in quite a small area of the continent. On the other hand, it should not be forgotten that the alchemists, on writing down their dark treaties, full of images, used to a large extent mythological and symbolic devices that were already found in the epic traditions of the West. The famous ecstasy in Peredur before the crow that*

121

drank blood in snow come primarily from a purely Celtic poetic image, there is evidence that it was used in Ireland long before this time. Was this a coincidence? Maybe, but we can also talk about the merging of two schools of impregnable thought given that, like the alchemist texts, the Celtic ones, often have two or three meanings. The same happens with traditional writings.

Therefore, the meaning of the quest is not alchemist in its totality, and is not based on pure shamanism. The hero of the Grail is too busy with himself to be manipulated by a set of compulsory problems: In the beginning, Peredur-Perceval was a 'fool' who sharpened his wits adventure after adventure, but he himself had no idea of the quest that he was undertaking. His wandering is anarchic as he never knew where he was going: he did not even know what he wanted: to go back to his mother, to experience adventures, or go back to White Flower. He forgot everything at the time of the Procession of the Grail, and he needed to be reminded. What is more, he was losing his way even more. He was not really under the impression that the original scheme of the search is constructed on an imperturbable structure. In a certain sense, Peredur-Perceval could be said to be a poet primarily, a dreamer; maybe it was what gave him strength.

As a dreamer, Peredur-Perceval is comparable to a shaman. The scenery of his exploits was, above all, a dream universe and not a real universe that is perfectly locatable. In short, everything happened in his mind and so the range of events described in the quest should not be taken literally.

The importance of blood

The adventures showed that the quest for the Holy Grail was going to be spattered with blood. The knights were not educated to engage in dialogue with the enemy with the intention of finding a peaceful agreement. The words that were exchanged consisted of threats or a kind of trick but this never prevented the crossing of swords.

Blood was present in society in the Middle Ages as wars were continual and most of the population lived and died by military dictates. Soldiers were permanently being recruited, as even the most minor nobleman had his army. So killing the enemy in an extremely bloody way was part of this setting. However, we should not overlook the fact that blood constituted the basis of the major religions: the Jews conferred a leading role upon it at the Last Supper, which is why it is used in the most poignant part of their services. Some drops of Jesus Christ's blood were placed in the Grail.

The divine blood sought peace, brotherhood, although, in his name, crusades were being organized against the infidels. The peaceful sense of brotherhood had been forgotten. The quest for the Grail required weapons to spill blood, which, in essence, fuelled the hero's reputation, because the dead person whose blood had been shed was generally a tyrant that oppressed a lady or an entire region.

Intuition is preferred

Aside from his weaponry and horse handling, the hero is portrayed as an ordinary man. He is rarely excessively intelligent and in certain cases he is dim. He had a noble intuition that allowed him to gain victories, which, in turn, make him stand out against other men. The fact that most of his victories were bloody would not be an obstacle to his being idealized in the end.

The authors that shaped Grail literature had the ability to convey to the male reader of that time, and on another dimension to today's also, the idea that he could do likewise. The hero doubted on many occasions, he hesitated on a few and he always showed that the obstacle could have proved too much for him: yet he acted and was successful. He was never vain as he was continually accompanied by the human concern of failure.

The adventure was further complicated by mystery and strangeness to create a tangle that was never completely unravelled, even though the hero was unscathed by events. We must bear in mind that writers were handling odd concepts, some of which were pagan and concealed in fables as it was the only to evade censure. The prince or nobleman, fulfilling his role as patron of the arts, read the work, sometimes in the close presence of a member of the clergy and its content could not be displeasing to him.

Mystery always followed the hero, and on many occasions it came in the form of a beautiful lady.

If from the outset the poems or novels the patrons of the arts were funding were supposed to highlight their house or family, as promoters of major national or international enterprises, there was also an attempt at conveying a religious message. Adventure was made use of for this purpose, naturally of Celtic inspiration with pagan roots. Hiding this influence meant complicating the plot, overdoing the mystery and leaving situations unresolved to give the censor peace of mind. Furthermore, the hero was young, rather naïve, free of malice and very intuitive, like many biblical characters or certain saints, but the author introduced his own variants, not forgetting esotericism or profane love.

Let us return to the Celts

The Celts did not usually differentiate between friend and enemy or two opposing forces, as they were two sides of the same coin. Life led inexorably to death, but when it came, a birth was taking place somewhere else, which hopefully served to regenerate the race. From an existential standpoint, though different, the body and mind are also complements, yet this is not true on a materialistic level. The body could, at no time, live without the spirit. Celtic legends were based on this concept and conveyed it through the medium of the symbolic adventures of some heaven-sent heroes.

We have also examined Celtic literature on the Grail and have seen that the main characters were portrayed as normal men. Even the gods acted as if they were stuck on earthly customs. Yet this was fully intended by the wise Druids, the priest-magicians of the Celts, with the aim of making their teachings more accessible. They were masters educated in the woods, friends of Nature, and spoke in terms that everybody could understand.

Capitalizing on the essence of communication available in Celtic legends the Christian religion could base their Grail stories on them. Chrétien de Troyes is not thought to have been influenced by the Church when writing his poem about Perceval; however, in view of the success of his works, some of those that were 'plagiarized' started to have the Christian message introduced into them.

The simplest of messages

A close analysis of the stories about the Holy Grail shows that there is no pattern to its appearance. On some occasions the hero leading the quest was close to the castle housing the sacred vessel and did not realize. On others, he needed someone to tell him as he could not find it randomly.

The message it aims to convey is very simple: go away from the place where you live because, from this distance, you might see that the treasure you were looking for is in your house or right in front of you, but you could not see it. This message has given rise to some beautiful fables such as the following:

One night, an inhabitant of Baghdad woke up restlessly because he had just dreamt that there was treasure hidden in the city Cairo. He had just 'seen' it so clearly that he thought it had to be true. As he was an astute man he exchanged his clothes of a rich merchant for those of a pauper in the hope of being less conspicuous. He managed to scale the walls surrounding Cairo without the guards bothering him; but, he loitered around the place where he knew the treasure to be for so long that in the end he was arrested, as he was thought to be a thief planning a new misdemeanour.

When he was in his cell, he voiced his innocence so sincerely that the police deputy decided to listen to him. The officer then found out that there was treasure hidden in a house in Cairo. The impostor described the house in such detail that the police deputy realized it was his. That night he dug up his own garden exactly where the prisoner had told him and, indeed, he found the treasure…

The key to the mystery is: what is really important often lies within yourself or in your immediate surroundings, but it has become so commonplace that it is concealed. The person needs to have his eyes opened by something or someone. This is the message that the quest for the Holy Grail tried to convey.

Was the quest within everyone's reach?

Anyone could be triumphant in his quest for the Holy Grail. At least that is what is implied in the poems and novels. Nevertheless, as the troubadour Thibaud de Champagne wrote: *The messengers are lit up at night and during the day are invisible to men.* In fact, everything contained in the writing is symbolic. Exposing oneself to the dangers of riding in the dark is the only way of finding the true path.

Based on this, scholars, philosophers and saints are frequently portrayed as blind people in need of someone to light the way. In Grail literature, the so-called 'Night Sun' is never the same as daytime sun, as its glare is brighter allowing the hero to 'see' like a shaman, a druid or a magician: they are the eyes of intelligence or the spirit.

The quest for the Grail represents a climax in human thought, one of the privileged cultural landmarks that should be maintained forever. Yet on some occasions, even sublime great heroes failed in their attempt to succeed in this most noble of ventures.

The exalted moment

In the third part of the *Conte du Graal*, Manessier described the exalted moment when the Grail was found in this emotional way:

... All the knights and ladies took Perceval's weapons from him with great joy and he stood beside the king who loved him so much that he called him son and friend; Perceval held this deserving man, who he had served so loyally, in the greatest esteem. Without waiting a second longer, the king ordered the tables to be set, and for it to be done quickly. They placed table-cloths, knives and salt cellars on them and once they had washed their hands they sat down and the king sat next to Perceval.

Then the lance appeared, as did the Grail, carried by two maidens who behaved with great delicacy, and when they passed in front of the tables they were all crammed with delicious dishes. Then the maidens carrying the Grail and the lance swiftly returned to the chamber they had come from. There they stayed for a while before returning to the room they had just left in the same way. All those sitting at the table satisfied their hunger and thirst and when they had finished doing so the Grail and Holy Lance went by, with its white iron shaft from which welled a drop of blood. Next a noble page appeared carrying a silver platter covered with beautiful, rich linen of reddish silk. They walked in front of the tables before returning to the chamber.

The Welshman gazed at them so hard he forgot to eat the three times that the Grail went by the table, and all those present, including Perceval, saw it clearly. They also saw that after the Grail a platter and the Holy Lance were taken to the head of the table where Perceval and the king were sitting and then returned to the chamber as they had done previously. Those sitting at the table ate heartily until they were satisfied; afterwards they washed and got up from the table. And the king, enflamed by these heroic deeds, took Perceval's hand and led him to one of the windows to say to him:

My good kind friend, you have gone through great hardship to rid me of this torment, which would never have ended in all the days of my life were it not for you. I do not know your name yet and I want to announce the good you have done for me in many far off countries. Be so good as to tell me your name.

And Perceval in turn said to him:

Sir, my name is Perceval the Welshman, never have I hidden my name, I was born and bred in Wales but since I received my weapons I have not been back to my country. I do not know my father's name, but I know for certain that my mother was the lady of the Barren Forest. Against her will I went hurriedly and resolutely to the court of King Arthur to ask for weapons. Then, I went to many countries and I searched and conquered many lands.

You certainly have a good reputation*," said the Fisher King.* But my Lord. Tell me, Agloval Gragonial the Welshman, is he your brother?

Yes, Sir.

I am glad, *said the king.* You are my nephew, I know for certain and your mother was my sister, a lady with a very noble heart, the most upright and prudent of our lineage; she died of sorrow by the bridge because of you. But now I am content and I thank God for seeing you here completely sound. From this moment on, all my lands are yours; As God is my witness, come what may, I shall make you king at Pentecost, without anyone opposing or contradicting me, it will be as I have said.

Perceval sighing answered him:

Sir, as I am your nephew, I swear to God, I shall not wear the crown on my head nor shall I be King while God gives me life; I do not want your lands. If you need me I shall not be so far that I cannot come promptly, no obstacle shall hold me back, unless it is prison, illness or death. I do not know what else to say to you as by Saint Martin I must go tomorrow to the court of good King Arthur, but I will see you again if God who rewards with goods gives me strength to do it.

All present were delighted by Perceval's revenge on Goon of the Desert, lord and king of the desert; they also were very glad when the king told them with great joy that Perceval the Welshman was his sister's son. The two cousins showed him their joy through the great pains they took to celebrate, and the party lasted until midnight when it was time to go to bed.

The king showed his love for his nephew by having him sleep by his side until the following day and granting him any other pleasure he desired, for having a loyal heart. As soon as dawn broke, Perceval got up and asked whoever had put his weapons away to bring them to him, but they were broken and in pieces, completely destroyed. The king made them bring the weapons that he had carried before being crippled; blacker than ink they were.

Good nephew *he said.* Please take these weapons for my sake, they are my royal weapons.

And without any further hesitation he put on his armour and mounted his white horse. He asked permission to leave like a polite and courteous gentleman, and armoured from head to toe he went through the gate bearing the weapons that were darker than blackberries...

Chapter XI

SIR LANCELOT OR THE GREAT
FAILURE

High quality literature

The work that has come to be known as 'Prose Lancelot' belongs to the Vulgate cycle and is made up of three parts: *Lancelot, Quest for the Holy Grail* and *Mort Arthur*. Probably written between 1215 and 1230, one creator laid down the general structure and another two or three shaped the work in accordance with literary guidelines. Gautier Map is possibly one of the creators involved. What we can be certain of is that the whole work was written on the properties of Henry II Plantagenet.

If we study the texts that give shape to Lancelot, his son Galahad and all the other characters, we notice a tendency for narrative boldness in dispersing the actions into a series of isolated sequences, which are then skilfully brought together to break, once again, the lineal storyline with some changes that enrich the plot as a whole.

'Prose Lancelot' is a kind of cathedral of Grail novels, in which there was no hesitancy in using any gothic resource, an artistic style that was not only prevalent in Europe through architectural forms. Although the Christian message was very present in the storyline, authors still focused on human beings, their complexes and the responsibility they assumed through simply being alive. A transcendental mission, such as the quest for the Holy Grail increased the degree of responsibility. Lancelot devoted himself heart and soul to this mission but he bore a heavy load, a sin, which he ended up paying for.

A knight of French origin

Lancelot is portrayed as a French knight born close to Bayonne (later we will offer another curious origin for this character) and was the son of King Ban de Benwick. He has several brothers and sisters, whom he lived with for a short time as the Lady of the Lake abducted him. She was so desperate on seeing that Heaven would not let her become pregnant that in the end she abducted the strongest and most beautiful child. She took care of this son in France and England and did not hide from him that he belonged to royalty.

However, when Lancelot arrived at the Court of King Arthur he was dressed humbly and never told anyone of his origins. He wanted to progress in life on account of his own merits, which he managed to do without too much difficulty, becoming one of the principal knights of the Round Table. He also eagerly fulfilled his role as an ambassador abroad. While he was carrying out his mission he travelled around the country where he was born, Christian Spain, and Italy.

On returning to England, he was accompanied by King Arthur. He immediately became his right-hand man; in the meanwhile, his reputation as an invincible knight started to take shape, to such an extent that nobody dared confront him, not even in training exercises. Furthermore, he became Queen Guinevere's best defender.

Later, Lancelot had to go on a journey, on this occasion, to inspect England itself. This allowed him to see for himself the mark that recent wars had left; some areas of England had been reduced to ruins. When he was staying at a fortified house one morning, while dozing, he suddenly heard a clash of metal and woke up. He looked out of the window and saw an armoured knight fighting with three bandits. He did not think twice in lowering himself down with a rope, after putting his armour on and taking up his sword.

Lancelot in the cart. Miniature of a French manuscript (National Library of Paris).

He only needed to deal three blows to scare the trio of wrongdoers, who then gave in. He saw that it was Sir Kay, King Arthur's brother. The next day Lancelot asked Kay to exchange suits of armour so he could continue his route without being bothered. As he accepted, the hero went on his way imagining that there would be many who would challenge him because they would not recognise him.

Chapel Perilous

In woodlands, Lancelot was actually assaulted by a lady. She asked him to help her brother Meliot de Logres who was in danger of bleeding to death at the Chapel Perilous. According to a witch, the only thing that could save him was a knight bold enough to take a sword and a piece of cloth away from under his body.

Lancelot realized that the wounded man was a knight from the Round Table, which increased, if possible, his desire to intervene as quickly as he could. He went to the Chapel Perilous. Facing the façade of the building, he was told amidst the presence of large number of lowered shields that his masters had been killed; furthermore, he considered a large number of the holders to be friends or companions.

Suddenly, he was surrounded by a group of sinister characters with a look of murderers about them. All wielded swords, and by the way they were acting they were convinced that he would be their next victim. He could not help giving a gesture of apprehension, which was as close a feeling to fear that he could experience. On entering the Chapel, he realized that the sinister company had vanished.

Once inside, the door closed behind him and everything became dark. After a short while, his eyes got used to the dark and through the dim light that remained he managed to see a body stretched out in front of the altar. He approached it slowly and touched the material the corpse was stretched out on. He cut a piece of it and suddenly the whole place was shaken by an unexpected earthquake.

Lancelot jumped to reach the dead body's sword. As he had the objects he needed, he attempted to leave Chapel Perilous. When he managed it, he found himself standing in front of the group of spectres, some of who were telling him to drop his sword if he wanted to stay alive. He paid no attention. After running around the graveyard, he found a strange woman standing in front of him, who also asked him for his sword. The hero refused so she asked him for a kiss, which he also denied her.

Then the unknown woman went red with anger and shouted that if Lancelot had given over his weapon and accepted the kiss he would have died like the other knights, as the Chapel Perilous was a death trap 'for heroes' that were passing by. Confronted by failure, she withdrew so the victor could look for the lady that awaited him.

Together they rode to the castle where Sir Meliot had almost bled to death. But the touch of the piece of cloth and sword healed him immediately. The witch's spells were also cancelled out so the spectres came back to life with the same vigour as before they had fallen into the trap. This event was recounted in King Arthur's court and added to Lancelot of the Lake's reputation.

The day Lancelot was left naked

Weeks later, King Arthur gave Lancelot the task of pacifying the region where the witch lived. The hero set out in that direction. One morning he heard the sound of bells that hunting falcons wore. It did not take him long to realize that one of these birds was caught up in the top of an elm tree. He did not feel like saving it. Then a lady came begging him to help her set the bird free from there because if he did not, her husband would kill it, and she felt responsible for what had happened.

Lancelot offered his services but was not very convinced. The lady helped him take off his suit of armour, without which the hero felt naked to all intents and purposes (we mean he was defenceless as he was wearing undergarments) and what is more, he no longer had his sword at his side. In this guise he started to climb the tree, and he did not take long to free the falcon. Next, he tied it to a dry branch he had just pulled off and he dropped it into the hands of the lady waiting below. But her evil smile revealed that danger was close by.

In fact, suddenly the lady's husband, Sir Phelot, appeared wearing his best suit of armour and wielding a sword, because he was ready to kill Lancelot, for whom he had set the trap. Aware of his reputation as an invincible man, he thought he could defeat him easily this way. The hero realized how delicate his position was and resorted to dialogue; while still thinking about how to defend himself. As he began his descent he found a thick branch that he pulled off with a tug. Calculating well the distances, he leaped and managed to land behind the treacherous knight and disarmed him with some very precise blows.

Once he saw he was on the ground with his head uncovered, he took him by the hair and mercilessly decapitated him. He had acted in accordance with the rules: a treacherous knight must be executed on the spot. The lady was terrified; nevertheless, she did not shout for help as she feared Lancelot, who had begun putting on his suit of armour. He then left, thanking the lord for having helped him come through the unusual adventure.

When he arrived at Camelot he found that everyone knew about his new exploits as Kay and Sir Meliot de Logres had taken the trouble to tell them. This meant that he was deemed to be the most courageous and highly regarded hero throughout Europe.

The meeting between two people in love

In *The Knight of the Cart*, Lancelot is portrayed as being excessively in love with Queen Guinevere, to such an extent that his passion finally exceeded the respect he was due to Arthur, the 'deceived' husband. The hero rescued the queen who had been abducted by Meleagant. Even so he caused her offence by transporting her in a cart, because this vehicle symbolized mobile gallows. The climax came when they agreed to meet the very same night...

On leaving, Lancelot was so overcome with happiness that he forgot all his emotional torments. To him that night came round very slowly and the day seemed to him, in his impatience, longer than a whole year.

When night finally fell, he feigned being tired, said that he had stayed up for too long and that he needed to sleep. But those that have done the same will understand why he was acting in such a way. He headed off in the direction of his bed to trick the people at the inn. In actual fact, it was not his bed that attracted him; for nothing in the world would he or could he lie down. Just the opposite, he got up quickly and made sure that outside there was no moon or stars and that all the torches, lamps and lanterns in the houses were out. He left taking great care not to attract the guards' attention, so they would be sure that he had slept in his bed all night.

Queen Guinevere kissing Lancelot. Miniature of a French manuscript (National Library of Paris).

He managed to reach the orchard quickly and without meeting anybody. Luck was on his side. A canvas wall surrounding the orchard had recently fallen down. He entered through the gap and hurried over to the window. Once there, silent, trying not to cough or sneeze, he waited for the queen to arrive. At last she appeared, not wearing a shirt or a dress; just a white tunic and a scarlet cloak over it. Lancelot, seeing her lean against the bars at her window, waved to her lovingly, and she immediately did likewise: as it was the same desire that attracted one to the other...

Bars cannot be a barrier

Then they were close together, holding each other's hands. But the fact that they could not get closer together caused them infinite sorrow; they cursed the iron bars that separated them. Lancelot declared then that if the queen agreed, the bars would not hold him back from being by her side for very long.

But can you not see, said the queen, *how solid these bars are. They cannot be twisted or broken by hands alone. You will never be able to pull them out.*

Madam, do not worry about it. I do not believe that a few pieces of iron are stronger than me. Nothing will stop me being by your side, only your will. If you give me your permission the road for me will have no obstacles; if on the other hand, my proposal does not please you. I would not do it for anything in the world.

Of course, I give you my consent. My will does not hold you back. But, in case you make noise, wait for me to go to my bed. What a catastrophe if the seneschal sleeping in that room were to wake up...and see me at my window!

Go back to your bed, madam, do not worry about the noise I shall make. I believe I can pull out these bars without too much difficulty and without anyone seeing.

On hearing that, the queen retired. Lancelot stood in front of the window. He gripped the bars and pulled them in all directions. He managed to bend them before finally pulling them out. But the iron was so strong that he cut his first finger to the nerve and broke the joint of the same finger on the other hand. However he did not even notice that he was injured and shedding blood as there was something else on his mind. In spite of its height, he got through the window quickly.

138

The adulterous meeting

After making sure that Keu was asleep, he went over to the queen's bed, filled with greater adoration than that inspired by the relics of a saint. The queen stretched out her arms and put them round him and squeezed him against her heart; afterwards, she enticed him to her bed, by her side and she gave him the sweetest of welcomes...But if the queen's love was immense, Lancelot's was a thousand times greater...

Lancelot had achieved his goal; the queen pleasantly welcomed his presence and his desire; he had her in his arms. They kissed and caressed each other so sweetly and softly that they felt more fortunate and happier than anyone ever. But on this matter I shall remain silent; there are things that ought not to be recounted. The most delicious of pleasures is what history tells us.

During the night, Lancelot had got drunk on voluptuous delights. But the cruel day snatched her from his arms. Like a martyr, he got up very early and left, as to him it was torture; his heart prompted him to stay at the queen's side... Finally, he turned towards the window, unaware that he had left signs of his presence behind him: the sheets stained with blood that must have come from his fingers. His soul was dying, sobbing and sighing.

The impossibility of arranging another meeting weighed heavily on his mind. In sadness, he walked past the window through which he had entered swollen with happiness. Even though he had deep wounds in his fingers, he managed to straighten the bars and set them back in place, so that nobody, from either side, could notice that they had been pulled out or twisted. Before leaving, he knelt down as if before an altar. Then full of great sadness, he departed. Without being discovered, meeting anyone along the way or waking anyone up he reached his room, he undressed and he lay down on his bed. It was only then that he saw the wounds in his fingers, but he was not surprised, as he understood that they were due to pulling out the iron bars from the window. But in all other respects he did not intend to complain: he would rather have had both his arms pulled off than to have been held back by the bars...

Lancelot's sublime passion

Nobody found out about the adulterous act because the queen carefully hid the sheets stained with blood and her own clothes, which were spattered with the marks of passionate embraces. King Arthur guessed it however, although he did not retaliate against Lancelot, his noblest knight, whom many considered to be 'sublime'.

It is worth briefly analysing the relationship between Queen Guinevere and Lancelot because it was born out of the platonic sentiment of a young knight 'purer than the angels', as far as sexuality was concerned, to become an overwhelming passion. It may be claimed that for him she was like his only religion, the highest trophy. Yet, from the night he succeeded, it did not happen again; she may have decided it had gone too far. He would remember those moments forever, which made him, through his sublime devotion, one of the most romantic and idealistic characters in universal literature.

Sir Lancelot in the chapel of the Holy Grail.

In his sleep he saw the Grail

However, Lancelot had let himself be dragged down by earthly pleasures, and the 'punishment' would be not to conquer the Grail. In "Morte d' Arthur" when he arrived at the cross-roads, he stopped to rest and then...

He fell asleep. In his restless sleep he saw two beautiful white horses go past him. In between them there was a stretcher carrying a wounded knight. When they were close to the crossroads, they stopped. Sir Lancelot looked at him because he was in the same position; he heard the knight say: Ay, good Lord, when will this sorrow leave me? And when will the Holy Vessel come my way to bless me? As I have been through a lot without committing any evil deed...

Sir Lancelot then saw a candelabra with six lights appear next to the cross indicating the crossroads. He was surprised not to have seen the person who had left it there. Immediately afterwards a silver table and a sacred vessel appeared... The knight sat up on his stretcher, cupped his hands and whispered: Good Lord, if you are here in this vessel, look how much I need to be healed. *He crawled over to the recipient, kissed it and was immediately healed, then he gave thanks.*

Lancelot watched the scene without reacting because he thought he was still asleep. He did not move either when the healed knight remarked to his squire that the man sitting at the foot of the tree must have been a great sinner as he had not paid tribute to the Grail. Then, as he had no sword or suit of armour, he took those of Lancelot; and he also took his horse.

At that instant Lancelot woke up and sat up mulling over what he had seen. He still thought he was dreaming when he heard a voice say Sir Lancelot, harder than a stone, bitterer than wood and more naked than the fig leaf you are; therefore, go, leave this sacred place. *Lancelot came back to life and no sooner had he seen that his horse, sword and suit of armour had disappeared than he understood that all he had seen had not been a dream. This led him to accept that he was too much of a sinner to complete the quest, which prompted him to say:*

All my great deeds with arms I did in the name of the queen, for her I fought, be it right or wrong. I never thought about God, only about gaining her adoration and being loved more.

141

In the end there was a reward

But Lancelot did not give up his quest for the Holy Grail although he doubted his merits to succeed. After various adventures he reached the very doors of the sacred chapel, and he could see it inside...

Then he saw half the chamber. He saw a silver table, and a divine vessel covered with a small red sheet and many angels above it... And in front of the altar there was a good man dressed as a priest and he seemed to be performing mass. Lancelot thought that there were other men there and that two were placing the youngest in the priest's hands, he then lifted him up... The priest impressed Lancelot on account of his being able to bear such a heavy weight... When nobody came forward to help him ...and there was a strong blast of air mixed with fire that hurt him... He fell and did not have the strength to get up and he lost the ability to move, see and hear...

Lancelot had not even been able to get close to the Grail since his good intentions were not considered sufficient. He continued to be a sinner, which made him the great loser. That is why we have devoted this entire chapter to him. Other knights, despite their longing, could not succeed in their quest yet in Lancelot's case, he was a hero, superior to the rest, and for him the great prize was out of reach as he had devoted all his attention to a woman, even though she was a queen, instead of to God.

As a kind of recompense, Lancelot's son, Galahad, was successful in his quest for the Holy Grail. He was the fruit of his relationship with Elaine, whom he slept with believing her to be Guinevere. An excellent lesson, in a literary sense, that leaves the reader, whether male or female, with a favourable impression.

If we look at 'Prose Lancelot', on the other hand, this work has been skilfully put together with a series of sequences and human beings, who slot into a perfect set. We have intentionally not followed this as we were more interested in writing about Lancelot to show an example of failure in the quest for the Grail.

142

Did Lancelot go to Galicia?

On hearing of our intention to research the subject of the Grail, a friend offered us a very curious little book by Rafael Usero, entitled *Sir Lanzarote do Lago e a sua proxenie Cedeiresa* ('Sir Lancelot of the Lake and his dear Cedeiresa'). It allowed us to gain an insight into Lancelot, who many authors call Lanzarote, as he belongs to a legend that says he visited Galicia. He stayed in La Coruña for a while when he was fleeing King Richard, who had ordered him to be killed on account of his relationship with Queen Guinevere.

The Knight of the Round Table lived in the village of Cedeiresa where he married the daughter of Count Rodrigo de Roma, with whom he had several children. Support comes for this from the fact that many people have the surname Lago, Spanish for 'lake'.

However, Rafael Usero carefully and elegantly pulled apart the legend. It should be recalled that in the thirteenth century the Pilgrims' Way of Saint James was already known; many stores reached Spain via this route, among them those relating to King Arthur and the Knights of the Round Table. Galicia always looked to England as they had been trading partners for a long time. The surname Lago could have arrived via these routes, later becoming a legend that many took as being true.

Seemingly, there was a time when parents liked naming their children after legendary characters. Is it too far-fetched to end up believing those characters had been in the villages of their most passionate admirers? Curiously enough, there is a coat of arms in Cedeiresa that is very similar to one used by the mythical Lancelot of the Lake.

This brief outline gives an idea of the strength that some legends can acquire, especially when accompanied by texts about key elements of the civilization at the time: politics and religion.

Let us return to the adventure

Although we did not initially intend to devote many lines to this chapter, we then decided to extend it to relate another of the

143

great failures of this hero, maybe the greatest of the knights that sat at the Round Table.

On the morning of the Feast of Pentecost, Camelot's celebrations were in full swing. King Arthur could not have been happier as he was surrounded by his most faithful servants. The announcement of a hermit's arrival did not take the smile away from his face. The banquet was under way and he thought that he would let the stranger take a seat at the table after telling him some prophecy.

However, the hermit wanted to appear before the Round Table and that was where they took him. Once he was in the impressive room, he pointed to the Siège Perilous and to King Arthur's astonishment, he said that he knew who was going to occupy it rightfully.

The King of Camelot shuddered, as he guessed what he was going to say next. In fact, the recently arrived hermit told him that Merlin the magician had died but that his soul had gone to the hermitage to talk to an old friend.

But, keep calm, Your Excellency, because the person who is to receive the great honour has not been born yet. I will tell you more: that knight will later conquer the Holy Grail.

The new prophecy left profound astonishment in the air: while, the person who had made the announcement turned to leave the castle. They did not stop him because it was thought that the Siège Perilous would be occupied much earlier. One of the fortunate ones should have been Lancelot of the Lake, however, they had just found out that was not to be the case.

The beautiful woman in the cauldron of boiling water

Lancelot returned to the paths as he had always done to impose law and order. A few days later, he scaled the walls that protected the hamlet of Carbonek to find himself surrounded by a crowd. A middle-aged man greeted him and then told him that they had been waiting for him to save them from danger: to get a beautiful woman out of a cauldron of boiling water. She had been subject to this martyrdom for years while the region suffered continual calamities, which was why they were convinced that the two punishments were linked to the same curse.

The noble knight was taken to a tower. One of its rooms had been closed off with a large iron door. Someone opened the lock and a cloud of steam immediately enveloped everyone. It took them a few seconds to make out what was in there.

Finally, Lancelot could a see young girl, completely naked, sitting inside a cauldron of boiling water. He did not hesitate in giving her his hand and in a moment they both managed to escape from there. Only a knight with a noble heart and proven judgement could break the curse.

A dragon with flaming jaws

The young girl told him that Queen Morgan la Fay and the Queen of North Wales were to blame for her punishment and the suffering of the region. All because they could not bear that she, Elaine, the daughter of King Pelles was the most beautiful woman in those lands. She had been waiting for a hero to release her for five years.

Elaine went off to the chapel to give thanks to God; yet, she was still looking around for Lancelot, with whom she had fallen madly in love. She did not smile and her eyes had that leaden look of afternoons when a storm is brewing, because she wanted the impossible. Everyone in the kingdom knew that he had given his heart to Queen Guinevere, whom he served with complete devotion.

When the religious service was over, the hamlet's inhabitants approached Lancelot to ask him to free them from another threat, for a terrible snake had taken over the graveyard and they could not go there for fear of being devoured. They immediately walked over to the graveyard, the site of the threat, on one of the gravestones somebody had written:

A leopard with royal blood shall stand before me, the only one that will succeed in overpowering the snake is now under this tombstone. The leopard will give life to a lion that will surpass all the knights in the world in nobility and honesty.

Lancelot did not have to rack his brains to find out that the writing referred to him as he was the son of a king and his shield bore a leopard.

The inhabitants stood back. The hero lifted the gravestone with one hand while holding his sword in the other. Suddenly the graveyard filled with cries of anguish because a flame-belching dragon had just appeared. It immediately looked for the knight at its side, who was trying to stab it with his sword. He did not harm the dragon, as its scales were as tough as steel and a few inches thick.

An added risk for the knight was that deadly tongue of flames that tried to reach him. He sought to defend himself with his shield, this time without using his sword but moving backwards all the time. In this way, he discovered a weak spot in the beast's body: and he drove the full force of his right arm into it. He could see the consequences and was satisfied to hear the agonizing roar of the dragon, which very soon was to render itself to its last convulsions.

While he was taking the sword out of the beast's body, Lancelot remembered the words written on the tombstone. The first part of the message had come true. But what did the second part mean? How could he interpret the message of ...*The leopard will give life to a lion that will surpass all the knights in the world in nobility and honesty*?

The brief appearance of the Holy Grail

The next day, King Pelles held a great feast in Lancelot's honour as he had freed them from immense danger. The most important people attended and the inhabitants of the hamlet were represented. Naturally, nobody attracted gazes like a hero dressed in all his splendour. Everyone wanted to congratulate him and then ask for consent to embrace him.

Oddly enough, Carbonek was a place where important relics were kept. At the height of the feast, when the toasts were about to be made, a white dove flew in through the large high up windows. Immediately it could be seen to be carrying gold censer. This was the preamble to a fascinating scene when the entire royal room was bathed in a delicious aroma and, at that moment, before each of the guests, a plate of their favourite food appeared.

Next, a virginal maiden appeared carrying a gold vessel. King Pelles approached her as he was the guardian of the relics and knelt down. Everybody followed suit; and then they began to pray. The maiden and the chalice immediately disappeared. The scene came to a climax when the monarch stood up, gave his hand to Lancelot to assist him and then, he told them what they had just witnessed, the most exalted spectacle: the presence of the Grail.

The seduction of Elaine

Elaine was falling more and more in love with Lancelot; and her passion was now so consuming that it knew no limits. As Dame Brisen, her lady-in-waiting, had been a sorceress with great powers, she begged her to use them to help her. There are skills that are never forgotten, and this is especially relevant to the most perverse ones. That is why the beautiful little lady could slip somebody a potion while chanting a spell. These were two magic elements that allowed her to act decisively.

During the dinner, the noble knight took Elaine by the arm, he took her to his room and he enjoyed himself with her. He was convinced that he was spending a second 'adulterous' night with Guinevere!

As the sly sorceress had left the room in semi-darkness, nobody bothered the lovers and the inevitable happened… a love scene like this one would make any story immortal, as long as it was not known that in the background betrayal was looming…

The moment of Lancelot's enlightenment

When the first rays of sunlight shone through the bedroom, Lancelot got up and went to open the window. He had always liked the air at dawn. No sooner had he felt its caress than the spell disappeared. When he reached the bed and saw Elaine, he realised he had been deceived. He thought he had spent the night with Guinevere and contemplating that young girl, despite her beauty…

He thought he had gone mad and put his hands to his temples as if his head was going to explode. He had broken all the promises he had made to the woman he idolized, he was not worthy of any respect, he had lost everything.

Suddenly, amid roars of anger, he took his sword out of his scabbard and raised it before the treacherous woman. He seemed willing to do it. Yet, at the moment of truth, he realized he could not go through with it and preferred to put on his suit of armour, find his horse and get away from there.

Sixteen years on

Lancelot returned to King Arthur's court where he tried to revert to his normal activities. It was a big effort but after a couple of months, he was back to his old self. As his rule stood, he did not have anything to do with any woman because his heart belonged to Queen Guinevere, whom would never cease to idolize, because he had placed her on a pedestal.

A year later, news reached Camelot that Elaine, King Pelles' daughter, had given birth to a strong little boy, whom she had named Galahad, Lancelot's first name. When Guinevere found out the news, she wanted to speak to her most faithful knight. They saw each other in her private rooms where the most terrible scene of jealousy broke out: the hero swore that he had been seduced with a potion; yet the queen did not believe him, because a knight was trained not to fall into such traps.

Lancelot suffered the consequences as he felt like a traitor. He took years to recover. He even took part in a gory battle, in which one of King Arthur's allies was Sir Pelles, who brought back bitter memories to him. When victory came, a celebration was held and Princess Elaine attended. As she wanted to claim her rights as 'Lancelot's wife' all the time, he never appeared.

However, while he was in hiding, people said that he was meeting up with Princess Elaine at night. So many people repeated the lie that Queen Guinevere ended up believing it. And she reproached the hero and he reacted by jumping out of a window, after being expelled from Camelot.

He went out of his mind and wandered around like a madman for two years. When he returned to the court, he had an opportunity to recover. That way he was ready for the big meeting...sixteen years after spending the night with Elaine, the mother, he had Galahad before him, the son of both!

He was a fully-fledged knight, in spite of only being fifteen; so noble and brave to be able sit on the Siège Perilous without the ground opening up beneath him and being swallowed up by the abysses of hell. The old hermit's prophecy had been fulfilled! Furthermore, we know he succeeded in his quest for the Holy Grail, unlike his father.

Chapter XII

THE GUARDIANS OF THE HOLY GRAIL

The founder of the Order of the Temple

Hugues de Payns shared his surname with the region where he was born. The precise date is unknown, but it is thought to be possibly around 1080. The information we have on him starts when he was an official in a Champagne house. He probably had an important position, as two documents found in the archives of the Count of Troues carried Hugues de Payns' signature.

It is also known that he participated in the first crusade as one of the leaders of the army of the Count of Blois and Champagne. His show of bravery and articulate manner enabled him to establish a certain friendship with Godefroi de Bouillon and, later, with his two brothers: Baldwin and Eustachius of Bologna.

At the same time he met their cousin: Baldwin of Burgundy, Count of Edesa, who in time was to become Baldwin II of Jerusalem. All those contacts turned out to be vital for Hugues de Payns' future.

Years later, he returned to the Orient as one of Hugues de Champagne's captains. By that time he was already married, and had a son, Theobald, who in time was to become abbot of the Cistercian monastery of Sainte-Colombe-de-Sens.

In 1118, Hugues de Payns and eight knights, *who were all God fearing*, stood before Baldwin II who had just been crowned King of Jerusalem. They had not forgotten their past friendship.

Majesty, we have come to offer you our services as guardians of the pilgrimage between Jaffa and this holy city over which you reign, said the French knight, kneeling down on one knee. *Let me explain: we have studied this land very carefully, we know the Arab language and we shall not do anything without your authorization.*

You already have it, my brother, the monarch answered, without needing to look to his advisors. *You have arrived at the most opportune moment as many human lives are being lost at this crossroads.*

Those nine 'warrior monks' were treated as the most honoured guests and, the next morning, they received the gift of a permanent residence on the far side of the palace. It took up almost the whole of Solomon's temple. Some days later, the religious men who had the Holy Sepulchre in their custody gave them a piece of land next to their own.

As Hugues de Payns and his eight companions were in possession of almost the whole of the ancient temple of Solomon, they were given the name of Knights of the Temple.

They were soon to act as defenders of the highways, without having to draw their swords from their scabbards as their mere presence was enough to discourage attackers. They also had the support of the patriarch of Jerusalem, Gormond de Piquigny before whom they had made the three usual vows for monks: poverty, chastity and obedience.

Such a degree of submission for strong and healthy and intelligent knights was not natural though, as any of them would have achieved a larger fortune crossing the Pyrenees, given that they were all French, to offer their services to any of the kings or counts who for years had been fighting against the Moors, who still occupied more than half of Spain. Many had put their swords and horses to the service of causes like this one as there are testimonies giving evidence of the involvement of international mercenaries in the first years of the Spanish Reconquest. Hundreds of hamlets, villages and towns conserve proof of this.

This is why we should look into this first enigma, that has the backing of some historians such as Louis Charpentier, author of *The Mystery of the Cathedrals:* would they not be there looking for the Ark of the Covenant and the Tablets of the Law? These were two religious jewels that could grant their holders immortality and the power to dominate men.

This is a difficult question to answer. However, several voices of rabbi elders had contended that the treasures were to be found in the Temple of Solomon...Were they found by the first Templars?

Nine years later, Hugues de Payns and five of his companions travelled to France, as they needed to obtain support to found their Order with as much backing as possible. They were carrying letters of recommendation from Baldwin II who was funding the journey, and by this time they were not unknown people in the Holy Land.

The Templars were rendering great services to the pilgrims, they were receiving an increasing number of donations and already had a reputation for the ease with which they made friends both with Christians and the infidels. Many Arab sultans and emirs feared them.

Is it possible that there were not just nine of them, as historians endeavoured to claim, but many more? If we look at their interventions in the pilgrimage from Jaffa to Jerusalem or the many times that they successfully helped the army of Baldwin II, it is impossible to accept that such a small number of Templars could have done these things.

The Council of Troyes

In 1127, Hugues de Payns had the support of Father Bernard of Clairvaux, the future Saint Bernard, who persuaded Pope Honorius II to organise the Council of Troyes with the sole aim of authorizing the founding of the Order of the Temple. Nothing like this had ever happened before.

Two archbishops, ten bishops, seven abbots, two scholars and a multitude of other ecclesiastical figures attended. It was presided over by the cardinal legate Matthew of Albano, but the most frequently heard voice there was that of Abbot Bernard, as almost all the people attending had ties, in one way or another, with this skilful and wise cleric. That is why he could pull strings in the most advantageous way for the benefit of Hugues de Payns.

Naturally, he knew how to show off his articulate nature to the best before such an important assembly of theologists and important gentlemen of the Church. He expounded the principles and the first services of the Order before readily answering questions, yet he showed a skill found only in a master of men. This facilitated the founding of the Order of the Temple.

The Church needed to take up the sword

By having the Order of warrior monks, the Church had accepted the utility of taking up the sword, although its doctrine obliged it *to turn the other cheek in the face of an enemy*. The Arabs had taken Jerusalem, then blocked passage to the Holy Places. Crusades had been organised to recover those lands, and it could go much further.

The authorization of the Order of the Temple or the Templars was highly criticised by various religions groups who previously voiced their disapproval of the Pope preaching the Holy War. However opposition to this *armed wing of Christianity* lacked strength vis-à-vis the support it received from all European monarchs.

The Templars received almost full autonomy, as they were answerable only to the Pope. They could have convent-barracks, their own treasury and function in accordance with rules which were very different from those of any other religious order, in spite of them imposing poverty and chastity on themselves.

The life of the military order lasted fewer than two hundred years, but in that time they had managed to amass an incalculable fortune, having their own fleet of ships and their power extended almost all over Europe. They were especially strong in Spain, where they had proved to be the most effective military force against the Moors who still occupied more than half the peninsula.

The Orders were created to be destroyed

When the Order of the Temple became too powerful it became the eye of the hurricane, since it had made many mistakes, although these did not amount to a fraction of its successes. They were skilfully exploited by its enemies, especially by the French King, Philip 'the Fair', who, together with the Pope as an accomplice, put an end to all the Templars in one of the many genocides that have had the backing of both the Crown and the Church.

In the foreground, a Templar in his impressive clothing. Behind, two religious men from non-military orders.

Years later, in 1258, the Order of Saint John suffered a similar fate, under the accusation of abuse and alleged betrayals, whilst in 1307, the Teutonic Knights were to follow after being reproved by the Archbishop of Riga, although in this case, most of the members saved themselves. It was to be said that the knightly orders were created to be destroyed, especially when they could be seen to have grown too powerful and, most dangerously, to enjoy full independence.

The fight against the Templars could also be perceived as a fight against the Grail. The similarity between the Knights of the Grail and the members of the Order of the Temple was very obvious, especially to Wolfram von Eschenbach. He brought them into his works as the custodians of the Chapel of the Grail. Other authors preferred to portray the custodians of the Sacred Vessel as ascetic warriors, who wore white tunics bearing a red cross, a feature clearly identified with the Templars.

Joseph of Arimathea was said to have given Evelach, an ancestor of Lancelot and Galahad, a white shield with a reddish coloured cross, the same cross that Pope Eugenius III gave exclusively to the Templars in 1147. On the other hand, a ship bearing this standard picked Parsifal up to take him to a mysterious place where the Holy Grail had been deposited.

The true mission of the Templars

The Knights Templar as an Order regarded the 'holy war' as a form of devotion and freedom. It represented Christendom whilst having its own cult, in which they were not obedient to Jesus Christ. The idea of authority had also been displaced from Rome to themselves.

Such conduct was manifest in the records of the Inquisition. Although reliability is an issue as confessions were obtained under merciless torture; in the end, the prisoner said what the executioner wanted to hear.

It is not our intention to idealize the Templars, especially in view of their importance. At the height of their power they had over nine thousand different centres. One of their supreme leaders was the Great Master Gerard de Ridfort (1184-1189). He was a manipulator unworthy of the position he held. What we are going to relate should not be applied to all the components of the Order of the Temple, but to a hierarchy, which, as had already happened in similar cases, did not necessarily coincide

156

with the official visible one. For this purpose, it is sufficient to characterize the Templars.

Now we know that they had secret initiation rituals. To gain acceptance, the new convert was forced to reject the Cross, to the point of treading and spitting on it. He was then warned *not to believe in Jesus Christ, but in the Lord who was in Heaven*. Furthermore, he was told that Jesus Christ was a false prophet who had never been a divine being, sacrificed to redeem the sins of mankind, but a man convicted for his many crimes.

The main ritual the Order of the Temple had was performed on Good Friday, a key date for the heroes who found the Holy Grail, as the castle or chapel where it was kept was totally accessible on that day.

Had they been 'poisoned' by Islam?

One of the accusations that weighed on the last Templars was that they had treated some of the sacraments with disdain, especially confession and penitence, that is, those that went against 'sin' and 'atonement'. Furthermore they did not recognise the authority of the Pope or the Church and paid lip service to Christian precepts.

Seemingly, one of their main offences was that they had maintained a secret pact with the Muslims since their arrival in the Holy Land. This influence ended up having a firm hold over them; they had been 'poisoned' by Islam. We should bear in mind that the Templars were never a group of preachers, but warriors in permanent action. They lived few years in peace, as they were practically always fighting. As they proved very effective through knowing the ground perfectly, they were soon imitated.

The Arabs established the Order of the Ismaelites, an exact replica of the Templars, even to the point of having a double hierarchy: one visible and the other secret. It was also about to collapse when it was accused of not adhering to the holy texts.

Curiously, the Templars and Ismaelites both had red and white uniforms. The Templars wore a cross and cloak while the latter wore a sash and tunic. The supreme leader of the Ismaelites was the 'Lord of the Mountain' (Sheikh alyabal). He was their invisible master, in whose hands lay the life and death of the caliphs and sultans. 'Paradise' was the name given to him and his inaccessible residence and, strangely enough, the symbolism attached to it coincided with that used by the king of the Grail. One of the accusations that weighed on the Order of the Temple was that it had too close ties with the 'Lord of the Mountain'.

Philip 'the Fair' (left), the true person responsible for exterminating the Templars. But he would never have managed it without the complicity of Pope Clement V (right).

In the texts on the Grail foreigners were not despised, on the contrary, in many cases they were shown in a positive light. Wolfram von Eschenbach said he got his story *Parsival* from a pagan called Kyot, who lived in Toledo where there was a cabalist school. Parsifal's father fought under the orders of Saracen leaders. Joseph of Arimathea was an atheist until he was converted after enjoying the benefits of the Grail. He fought better than the infidel knight Firefiz. In short, this literature contains few differences in religious beliefs, as greater importance is placed on sin and purity, justice or injustice.

158

The panic of initiation

A Templar trial record states that a new convert was so panic-stricken as a result of initiation into the Order that his hair turned grey and so distressed that he felt his only way out was by committing suicide.

Certain knights that failed in their quest for the Holy Grail faced a similar ordeal: *the fear was so intense that their hair went grey and they were plunged into depths of incurable unhappiness.*

However, the panic experienced by the knights during their initiation as Templars was not caused by a sacred vessel but by the influence of a demonic figure, Bafomet. This idol represented carnality, immorality and the aberration of chastity. This monster had the bodies newborn babies, the fruit of relations between Templars and unknown women, burnt before him These women handed over their babies over, ashamed of having conceived them.

The shroud of Christ

Some historians claim that the Templars had an important religious relic in their custody, something maybe even greater than the Holy Grail. This relic was linked to the sacred vessel. Ian Wilson called the object that the Order kept in its moments of supreme power 'Madylion'. It consisted of a piece of cloth, folded several times and stretched over a wooden frame. It is believed to be the shroud of Christ that apparently had disappeared from the world during the siege of Constantinople in 1204; but it must have been a dangerous pretext to prevent it from falling into Muslim hands. Today the same relic is conserved in Turin cathedral and has been the subject matter of continual controversy and countless scientific investigations.

John Matthews in his book *The Grail: Quest for the Eternal* wrote the following:

If Wilson and Briggs are right, and there is no reason why they should not be, if the Templars possessed the religious relic, it would explain, to a certain extent, another of the 'blasphemies' they were accused of.

159

The blasphemy in question is the adoration of the self-styled idol called Bafomet (he was generally believed to have been corrupted by Mohammed), described as a bearded head with a crown. 'Mandylion' could easily have been misconstrued, as it is folded in such a way that only the bearded face of Christ with marks of the injuries inflicted by the crown of thorns could be seen.

There is an echo of this mysterious image both in the Grail account Perlesvaus and in the Cistercian-inspired Queste del Saint Graal, part of the Vulgate cycle and composed at the monastery of Saint Bernardo, in Clarivaux. In "Perlesvaus", King Arthur himself attended the mass of the Grail and when he looked towards the altar, He believed the hermit saint (who was performing mass) was holding a man in his hands. This man was bleeding from his side, the palms of his hands and soles of his feet and he was wearing a crown of thorns... Whereas in the Queste, Galahad attended mass held in the temple of Sarras, the Holy City of the Grail. The vessel was kept in a chest on a silver table, an image reflecting both the Temple of Solomon and the Holy Sepulchre, and figured in all the Templar headquarters in the world, and wherever the most sacred rituals were held.

Thus we have the Templars based at the Temple of Solomon, who guarded a sacred relic, professed special devotion to the Virgin and were backed by Saint Bernard; these are recognisable elements of the Grail traditions. Approved by the Pope, with their rules written by one of the leaders of the Church in Western Europe, for some time they held the highest earthly power. All western Christendom was accustomed to the idea of knights. The Templars were super knights who combined fighting skills with the spiritual fervour of priesthood. Therefore we should not be surprised that many Grail authors took the Order as a model not only for the knights of the Grail, but also for those of the Round Table.

The idea that excessive power contains the seeds of self-destruction is also evident here. Power can devote itself to the truth, but when the truth contains many errors it collapses. When the kingdom of Jerusalem had been assured, albeit precariously, the Templars, like the Round Table, fell apart. The accumulation of wealth and power only served to generate envy and fear. Earthly Jerusalem merely symbolized the celestial

*city; the discontentment engendered by the harsh times and out-
moded customs shook the high purposes that were the starting
point for the Crusades. As their earthly kingdom was consolidated, they lost sight of the celestial one. A scapegoat was needed and the Templars fitted the bill.*

*God's military order had been founded on the highest
Christian ideals, like the knights, which the leaders of the
Church of that time blessed. In an ironic twist, these men were
accused of the same evils as the Cathars: denying God, defama-
tion of the cross, veneration of false idols and the practising of
vices against nature.*

*In the light of the similarities between the accusations and
the confessions obtained under torture that both parties only
half understood we are tempted to believe that there is a body of
teachings capable of making the Templars the true inheritors of
the Catharian heresy. They had the same beliefs and objectives,
though perverted and twisted by the changeover from a passive
to an active role.*

Chapter XIII
THE TROUBADOURS AND THE CATHARS

'Love's faithful'

The troubadours were called 'Love's faithful' on account of their passion for 'idealizing' the relationship between a man and woman. They could be said to have introduced the importance of romance in the period leading up to marriage, from eleventh century. The sentiment of man's attraction for woman, considered almost as a religious ceremonial, in which he bends over backwards to show his best side, with the noble purpose of conquering 'the most beautiful and delicate creature'.

One of the clearest examples is found in Lancelot's absolute devotion to Guinevere, although she was another man's wife, and in this case the king of both of them. 'Love's faithful' did not discriminate between the married and the single woman, as the most exalted aspect of women was their beauty, not their marital status. Logically, one of the most highly praised qualities was youth, freshness, and this was usually an endowment more common in single women.

The Holy Grail could also be found by love, although it was a different type of love. It could be called a vocation of faith in God, to which the will was entirely devoted to the point of annulling one's own personal desires. So love acquired a divine 'dimension', and was represented by the Roman Church through monastic orders, be they Benedictines, Cistercians or Franciscans. In churches and abbeys, religious teachings were taken from sermons and commentaries on the Scriptures. The knights' undertaking in their quest for the Grail can also be considered a vocation.

The love of a lady

It is noteworthy that the first troubadours were Cathars for the most part. They lived in the South of France and created romantic poetry. We have memories or inheritance from them possibly because the Roman Church did not see any danger in allowing the verses to be known yet they were harshly criticized by some. However, the work of the 'good men', as the Cathars were also referred to, was wiped out and obliterated. What has been conserved has been drawn from a stone: extracted from secret archives and word of mouth. 'Manipulated' reports of the inquisitors have had to be 'turned around'.

Society's behaviour towards the troubadours left no room for doubt. They were welcomed everywhere they went. In many cases they informed others about what was happening in the world because castles in the Pyrenees were located in rocky places, barely accessible and therefore isolated. The ladies who resided in them lived for their beauty and they needed to be flattered by the singing poets.

There had previously been times of legends that skirted the truth. One narrated the tragic story of two lovers who were caught red-handed by the husband. He killed the 'attacker of his home' and then forced his wife to eat the heart, still warm, of the man who had loved and 'lost' her. The troubadours offered a less dramatic kind of love. Jaufre Rudel wrote:

> *I will never forget a distant lover...*
> *But I do not know when I will see my love*
> *I still believe in God's sincerity,*
> *That is why I will see my distant lover...*

This is pure poetry. Love is laden with sadness. He resorts to divinity and hopes for an ending that may never come. The outcome is left to the listener's imagination or lady that it has been devoted to. Jaufre Rudel wrote it for the Princess of Tripoli,

164

whom he had never seen, but news of her beauty had reached him. In the end when the character from the poem was very old he went and died in his lover's arms. Could there be more sublime evidence of platonic love?

A lady and a troubadour carved in marble. Sculpture from the thirteenth century conserved in the Museum of Cluny.

The verses therefore turned the lady into an unattainable ideal, proclaiming the following: *The sky must be reached for the love of a woman.* The poet Uc-de Saint-Circ used the same idea when writing:

You can take my life as homage, a beautifully compassionate life, as for you I will reach the sky that I long for...

They invented loving passion

Ladies in the south of France, who lived in the twelfth century when Catharism was at its peak, could marry two or three times, but that did not stop them having a lover. The Troubadours invited her to do so by making her a myth, a pure challenge, the goal of any feat. She could make a man a hero if he loved her, or drive him to suicide if he rejected her. Little did it serve him to refuse to accept his destiny.

Seen from a distance or analysed as an historical event, the troubadours unquestionably invented loving passion. It may be claimed that previously loving passion did not exist, but from that moment it acquired an official meaning, it was universalised. It was to accompany literature until our day, with such prolific periods as the one experienced in the nineteenth century, with the emergence of Romanticism.

Where did the troubadours come from?

The troubadours came from monasteries and convents. They were not priests but educated men. As they lived in the Pyrenees, they were easily in contact with the Moors, who transmitted to them certain ways of distributing rhymes and more fluent metrics. Muslim sophists were known to be very much like Cathars, as shown by the following religious concept:

Paradise for any faithful agnostic is his own body, and hell for the ignorant faithless man is equally in his own body.

The great Ibn Arabi wrote: *In every loved being, God is manifest in the look of whoever has given his heart over to loving passion.*

In this text alone the embryo of all the passionate love developed by the troubadours is found. They went further, possibly because they were in a society, the Catharian one, which allowed it. To a certain extent it *was* permitted: carnal sin could be committed as long as there was an intention to repent.

The eroticism of the troubadours

Idealizing women may have become a sublimation of the erotic charge. The noble lady was married and enjoyed a more or less secret lover. She also received a visit from 'good men'

166

who spoke to her of carnal sin and at the same time they invited her to free herself from it by becoming a 'believer'.

These ladies were in a country that had just emerged from a primitive state. In the beginning sexuality was understood as a need, almost similar to having to nourish oneself when hungry, an animal act. With the appearance of the troubadours' eroticism, the primary drive was contained and the need for beauty emerged, as did courting accompanied by words and the invitation to provoke the most burning desire.

Men and women were convinced they had to like each other, to engage each other visually and verbally as that was going to lead them to the closeness of lovers, almost without touching each other, palpitating beneath their clothes, looking at each other with an invitation to await the reward that was worth having. The animalistic attack and consented rape, were things of the past, to give way to an erotic courtship, to which the troubadours were accomplices for having made love sublime…Could there be anything greater in the world? Of course not!

At this moment it iks necessary to resort to a text by André Nataf, who wrote in his book *The Catharian Miracle:*

…*When we state that troubadours 'dominated' loving passion, the reader has to adopt the right perspective for himself, which is not one of rejection but, to the contrary, of eroticism.*

The 'idealisation' of women occurred on two levels, a projection of their state of mind and their sensuality.

…*For the moment the Lady in the Castle offers us a key. Let the reader imagine that her soul (the reader only knows her soul through hearsay) has been forgotten in a childhood memory relating to the story of the* Sleeping Beauty of the Wood. *He must believe, as in a game, that he is that troubadour or knight who must free her, must wake her up. There are countless perils lying in wait. He is unarmed. If he loses, he will die and his sexuality will die with him.*

To a sensual person, the golden rule is to spiritualise love. As Brahman said: All enjoyment, all pleasure is a divine experience.

But beware!

Whoever looks for love in the hope of enjoyment is a victim of desire. A wise person accepts sensual pleasures when they come along, but with a generous heart, never a victim of desire.

Portrait of Domingo de Guzmán painted by Guido of Siena in the thirteenth century.

If the Lover obeys this rule, the image of God that manifests itself in the look of every person in love is not the pleasure of the Oedipus complex of psychoanalysis. Saying 'yes' represents a divine reality, a conquest that brings human beings close to the sublime, to a level of infinite spirituality...

The troubadours even exclaimed a near holy phrase, not in the slightest worried by contradiction, *Chastity stems from love.* They were not referring to the mystical love that Saint Theresa felt for Jesus but to that born through the encounter between a man and woman. With this the foundations were laid for such immortal works as *Romeo and Juliet* in which the two great lovers reach death without barely knowing each other in terms of the flesh, because what mattered to them was the sentiment that united them. Possibly, the precious thought of knowing they had found their perfect love match was enough to satisfy them.

The Perfect Ones

The Cathars established themselves in the Pyrenees in the eleventh century, where they started to spread with such force that in the end they emptied the churches. They did so by preaching love and the belief that wealth was not essentially evil, as long as it was put to good use. As their message was received by human beings working on the land, tending the cattle or trading, they were surrounded by faithful followers, all of whom stopped attending Christian services, where priests were always threatening them with eternal punishment.

The Cathars disapproved of carnal pleasures and encouraged people to live a spiritual existence. In the noble aim of reconciling themselves with God they called their priests and priestesses the Perfect Ones. Another of the novelties that surprised people was the fact that women could hold such an important position within a religion, which did not happen in the Christian church.

Scholars have found many points of convergence between the Cathars' doctrine and the knights' dedication in their search for the Holy Grail. It is essential when looking into the Cathars' beliefs to forget all the fanaticism that came out of the records of the Inquisition. They never hated life, nor imposed unworkable sacrifices, such as giving up earthly goods to the point of reaching extreme poverty. Yet the anchorites and Christian monks did. They retreated to woods and deserts with nothing to feed off but roots, leaves and insects.

What people really feared was that they did not believe in God of Israel. According to them, he was brought into History to place a greater importance on Evil to the detriment of Good. For this religion, of Manichean origin, human beings were good by nature, and everything bad came to them through a sort of Shadows.

They were convinced that Humanity came about by accident, involving minuscule elements of the original light coming together. They accepted the existence of a Heaven, that man and woman were expelled from, yet were convinced that it was possible to return to it through a key furnished by the Grail. Those that attained the goal recovered their original lost innocence.

They began in Languedoc

The Cathars began to spread from the French bastion of Languedoc, where they encouraged the learning of music, medicine and philosophy with a strong oriental influence. There they organized schools that studied Arab and cabalist manuscripts. Nobody feared talking openly about religion, science or alchemy. As it was a very rich region they could import carpets, all types of ornaments, silks and jewels.

They also started to receive a large number of troubadours. Along with luxury, commonplace in prolonged periods of peace, a taste for poetry and music was encouraged. The best poets and prose-writers were in the castles in the Pyrenees, many of whom had been converted to Catharism. The noblest widows did likewise and they were granted the title of Perfect Ones, which allowed them to run sewing workshops and hospitals. Because Cathar priestesses, just like the priests or Perfect Ones, were always supposed to be active.

We are describing times of prosperity that allowed the Cathars to spread throughout the south-east of France until they reached the north of Italy and a large area of Germany. It was such a powerful influence that it scared Pope Innocence I. Soon Bernard of Clarivaux, the future Saint Bernard, started to speak out against what they considered to be the 'Catharian or Albigense heresy'. He dedicated himself to a campaign to eliminate these 'sinful ideas', but achieved little.

The great enemy

Catharism's great enemy was the Spaniard Domingo de Guzmán, later known as Saint Domingo. He founded the religious group the Dominicans and one of his main objectives was to combat Catharism. The opportunity came in 1208, when Pedro de Castelnau, a servant of the Pope, was murdered. As Raymond IV was blamed, the Count of Toulouse started the crusade against the Cathars. Some historians doubt the veracity of this accusation, preferring to see it as a self-interested distortion. The fact is that it gave rise to a genocide.

The King of France had long set his sights on Languedoc along with the whole region of the Pyrenees, as they formed a kind of independent county. On joining the crusade with a large army, he secured the recovery of this rich territory, which he had been hoping to conquer for many years.

Going into full detail of all the implications of the Catharian or Albigense crusade would take up a book (and has already been published in this collection, which we enthusiastically recommend). Therefore we will just say that thousands of homes were set alight and still more innocent people were killed in the blaze. Domingo de Guzmán's cruel threat hung over them:

As you refused the blessings of the Church, we will answer you with its scourge. We will stir up princes and prelates against you. Yours towers will be destroyed and your walls pulled down, and you will be reduced to slavery.

They actually went a little further than this, given that they killed them. But they also devastated entire cities, although the dwellers showed great heroism. The Cathar bishop by the name of Girard de Montefuiore, before being burnt at the stake is reported to have said:

I am not the only one the Holy Spirit is visiting. I have a large family on Earth, made up of numerous group of men, whom the Spirit enlightens on certain days and at time certain times.

These words could doubtless have come from the lips of the king of the Grail as he was also visited by the Holy Spirit as mentioned in the novel *Parzival* by Wolfram von Eschenbach, when in one of the passages a dove descends to leave the holy wafer on the stone of the Grail.

Montségur, one of the Grail temples

John Matthews in his work *The Grail: the Quest for the Eternal* tells us the following:

Certainly the idea of the Cathars possessing some form of insight into the Grail became a generally accepted fact, as shown by the incident that occurred during the final siege of Montségur, the great Cathar citadel in the Pyrenees and the one that held out longest against invading armies from the North.

Montségur, similar to Muntsalvache, was the name of the Grail mountain in the poem by Wolfram and in Titurel *by Arberech von Scharfenburg. It was governed by Countess Esclamonde de Foix, possibly the most famous of the beautiful female Perfect Ones. In effect, she was so respected that many refused to believe she was dead. It happened shortly before Montségur was destroyed. They thought she would sleep until judgement day in the caves that formed a labyrinth running along the side of the mountain below the castle. Furthermore, many identified her with Repanse de Schoye, the maiden of the Grail.*

It was in these circumstances that the aforementioned incident took place. During the long siege of Montségur, a member of the Esclamonde family, the extravagant Roger de Mirepoix, dressed in a white suit of armour, appeared at the walls of the citadel holding a gold-handled sword on high. Before this vision, many of the besiegers fled the castle in dread, believing that they were up against the Knight of the Grail.

Another story, probably apocryphal, describes how the original chalice of the Last Supper was hidden in the cave of Saint Juan de la Peña in 713 (although there is no suggestion of how it got there) by an Aragonese bishop called Audeberto. When Aragon was threatened by the Moors at the beginning of the twelfth century, the sacred cup was taken to the Pyrenees and entrusted to the Cathars. When they were almost entirely annihilated, the chalice was smuggled back into Spain and hidden in a cave again, this time under the protection of Martin 'the Humane', the then King of Aragon. In subsequent years, the chalice was identified with the one that was kept in the cathedral in Valencia, and also with the one the Queen of Sheba gave to Solomon as a gift. Although this story at first glance may seem unlikely, it is encircled with genuineness. We should also not underestimate the fact that this precious object was entrusted to the Cathars.

The Castle of Montségur was one of the Cathars' last bastions.

In time Montségur fell, its defenders were murdered or burnt outside its walls, without being given a trial. Even today the *place still has an atmosphere of horror, which many who have been there have bore witness to. If that was the home of the Grail, it has not retained any of its sanctity. However, according to the story, during the night before its fall, four of the Perfect Ones escaped over the city walls and went to the mountains, taking with them sacred books and other secret treasures, with the chalice believed to have been among them.*

Whether the Grail was taken or not is irrelevant to our argument. But, if some of the Perfect Ones escaped, which seems reasonable, they would have taken the secrets of their faith with them. Out of every hundred heretics that died, half of them escaped to the mountains, fleeing to Italy and Germany, where they probably scattered their treasures.

Still their doctrines remained alive; their perpetuation can be tracked through the extensive traditions of esoteric knowledge. According to these, some of the sacred books fell into the hands of the Rosicrucians. Knowledge was passed on about the church of love, as it has been called since then and for the coming centuries. Elements of Catharian belief were infiltrated into the Grail texts, for instance, in Chrétien de Troyes' Lancelot. *One of the main works that included the new ethic of courtesan love along with King Arthur's knights tells us that after Communion kisses of peace were exchanged, in accordance with the oriental ritual that the Cathars adopted in their sacrament of 'Manisola', the celebration of love, evoking the imagery of both the Last Supper and the banquet of the Holy Grail.*

Although they believed in the malignant nature of the flesh, the Cathars wanted to transcend their humanity to be at one with the true god of light and were also true adepts of love (not profane and sensual love that the troubadours sang of, but of a spiritual feat, differing greatly from that of the orthodox Christians). They were full of burning anguish that gave them enormous resistance (in fact, the Cathar ritual called 'endurance' included prolonged periods of fasting, sometimes leading to death. Through this ritual they were purified to become recipients of light). Apart from the chance to possess the Grail, they did this for the sake God's love, the Light and being united with their universal brotherhood.

The Cathars may well have understood the Grail's message of love better than anyone else, as it was the overriding aspect of service and devotion to the Light. They carried with them the gospel, which contained knowledge of that light, but only the Gospel of John. In it they read the divine commandment that God was love, and being with him meant living in love.

Chapter XIV

THE GRAIL IN SPAIN

The Grail of Saint Lawrence

To a large number of Spaniards there is no debate about the Grail's hiding place or the route taken by its carriers. They are convinced that it has been in a gothic chapel in Valencia since the fifteenth century. The most fervent followers of this idea are the members of the Brotherhood of the Holy Chalice, who are in charge of its custody.

Yet the most scrupulous historians are not so bold, especially considering that there are more than thirteen chalices of the Last Supper. Almost since it began, the Church has supported the existence of sacred objects and relics, giving rise to the existence of an exaggerated number of chalices. The same goes for the wood from which the Cross was made; over twenty crosses, the same size as the original, could be reconstructed. The same can be said about the nails, the crown of thorns and so many other things. If we can believe the strange case of the *milk from the Virgen's breasts when breastfeeding her son Jesus* is kept in some chapels, we can believe anything. All we have to do is imagine that an angel brought it, or that a miracle occurred, to understand the faith of believers.

The Grails in existence

To the Church, the Grail is the chalice of the Last Supper. Its leaders should have felt compelled to carry out a scrupulous study to find out which of the ones in existence is the real one. This is a very difficult task if we consider what happened in the Middle Ages and then what took place over subsequent periods.

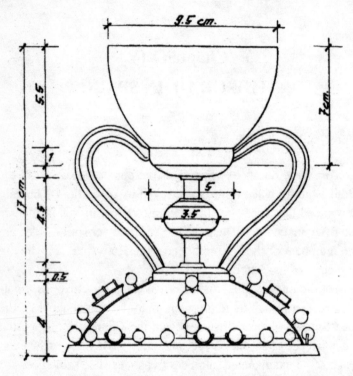

Dimensions of the Holy Chalice or the Grail that is conserved in Valencia (taken by Antonio Beltrán).

We have already said that one of the Spanish grails is in Valencia. It had to travel a long way before reaching its destiny. Apparently, Pope Sixtus II gave it to the deacon Lawrence to defend before finally leaving it in Huesca, his home town. It remained there for a long time, in fact, until it came under Muslim threat. They had just made their first conquests on

Spanish soil and it was this that prompted Bishop Auduberto to protect it. In his flight, the safest place he found was the monastery of Saint Juan de la Peña and this has been proved by a host of writers. In the mid fourteenth century, Martin 'the Humane' claimed it to take it to the Moorish palace of Aljafería, in Saragossa. From there, he completed the last leg reaching Valencia, at the request of Alfonso 'the Magnanimous'.

In England there is another Grail. It was stolen from an archaeological dig that was being carried out at Glastonbury and consists of a tray made of stone crystal, which can hardly be regarded as a chalice.

There is also an Italian Grail kept in Genoa cathedral. Its faithful call it 'sacro catino' ('holy bowl or basin'). According to the story, crusaders brought it from Palestine as their best conquest. They saved if from being stolen by the Arabs, who took possession of Jerusalem shortly afterwards, converted the cathedral into a mosque and then went on to take the Holy Land.

Did the Grail form part of the Catharian treasure?

Archaeologists have looked for shreds of evidence of the Grail's presence in countless mountains all over the Middle East and Europe. According to a Christian legend dating back to the thirteenth century, a pagan monument, situated in an inaccessible place destroyed in the seventh century, was home to the Grail. On this basis, the conclusion was drawn that an old Mazdaist temple was the point of reference.

We can accept, as a hypothesis, that the Catholic crusaders, who exterminated the Catharian heresy, firmly believed, maybe even had real evidence, that the 'good men' had the Grail, that it was part of their treasure, but they managed to get this treasure out of the castle of Montségur before it was forcefully vacated.

The Cathars may have taken the Grail to the Pyrenees, where they hid it somewhere so secret that only a few knew its precise location. As they died, a piece of information was lost that thousands of researchers and adventures have aimed to obtain regardless of cost and effort. We have already mentioned the Nazis, following the writings of Otto Rahn.

The many Spanish routes

The first routes taken by the chalice carriers inside Spain went through Huesca, Jaca, Yebra, Saint Pedro de Siresa and also San Juan de la Peña, where the best documentation is conserved in the monastery. Its church, built during the time of the Visigoths, brings together many centuries of important art and religion.

Juan García Atienza points out that at this church, burials have great importance. If it was the wish of famous personalities to be buried there in such a holy place, we are tempted to believe that it was because the Grail was kept there.

Knights of San Juan was the name given to an Order founded by some Aragonese warriors at this monastery. On their chests they wore a cross very similar to that of the Templars, further proof that the Grail must have been kept in this religious building, and why it was used to host a whole range of political, military and religious events.

One of the leading defenders of San Juan de la Peña as home to the Grail, was José Luis Solano. This is only natural given that he was the guide and guardian of the monastery. Thanks to him we know that many specialists visited the site, and some books kept there prove it. One of them under the title of *Le roman de Graal originaire* by André de Mandach aims to show that the characters in the poems by the Frenchman Chrétien de Troyes and those by the German Wolfram von Eschenbach were based on Aragonese kings, even though they gave them a British or English identity.

This French author went further as he claims that the Fisher King, the guardian of the Grail was in fact Alfonso I 'the Battler', the king of Aragon and Navarre. He opened a saga in which Perceval or Parsival and all the Knights of the Round Table participated. This is possible, as long as we accept that King Arthur, Camelot and the rest form part of a myth that has been reconstructed in such a way as to seem true.

The Aragonese Grail would lie very close to the Catharian Grail as both were located in the Pyrenees. Strangely enough, it cannot be situated exactly due to this right is 'disputed' by Aragon, Languedoc, Catalonia and even Galicia. Not to mention

Toledo, as Wolfram von Eschenbach says in an account that he obtained the manuscript for his work "Perceval" from this city.

Jaca refuses to be relegated

Allegedly, the beautiful cathedral of the town of Jaca, so mistreated by civil architects for having left it boxed in, was also home to the Grail. Defenders of this idea refuse to be left out of the Grail tradition, as they believe that they are just as entitled as anyone to make this claim if not more so. They claim that the entire monumental building was built to house the chalice of the Last Supper.

This treasure is not in the cathedral's archaeological museum, but other important historical pieces are, many of them having an esoteric meaning relevant to the Grail. The body of Saint Orosia, Princess of Bohemia (some say Aquitaine or Cordova) is worth a mention. She was beheaded by the Saracens after apparently arriving in Jaca to marry a nobleman, but died a virgin by some miracle. Her corpse was found in a cavern, after an angel had appeared to a shepherd to show him where he had to look. A long time before that, the Grail had been hidden in the exact same cave.

The head of Saint Orosia, patron saint of Jaca, is at Yebra de Bassa, where it is conserved, coated with silver gilt and wearing a crown and jewellery.

The Grail could have been at Montserrat

In the thirteenth and nineteenth centuries, German and Austrian authors such as Schiller, Humboldt, Goethe and others constructed a very impressive legend, which had all the makings of being true. This legend concerned Mount Montserrat, the centre of Catalonian religiousness. Richard Wagner introduced this idea in his operas *Parsifal* and *Lohengrin*.

The belief had gathered such support that on 23rd October, 1940, Heinrich Himmler, one of the supreme leaders of the Third Reich, arrived at the Benedictine abbey in Montserrat expecting to be handed a set of documents on the Grail. We have already seen, when discussing Otto Rahn, what the Nazis aimed to achieve with the sacred vessel. However, Father Andrés

Ripoll, who was in charge of the religious site, could not satisfy the German leader's request because he was not aware that the documents requested actually existed.

The old monastery of San Juan de la Peña, where the Grail could have been kept for many years.

Many years later it was discovered that the monks kept a very remarkable book in the library entitled *Montserrat, Ganga del Grial* by Ramon Ramonet Riu. In it the author affirmed that *Mount Montserrat provided the ore stone that accompanied the Holy Grail, that incomparable spiritual gem.*

Versed in the art of describing bold claims, we cannot consider this one to be inaccurate due to lack of scientific evidence proving the others to be true. The author suggests that Merlin was Count Arnau, and Lohengrin a pseudonym for Ramón Bereguer while King Arthur was really Wilfred 'the Hairy', the first independent Count of Barcelona.

The Grail tradition

Juan Garcia Atienza is the Spanish leading light on the fascinating subject of the Grail. In his *Guia de la España griálica* he says the following:

It may be necessary to point out that Spain is connected in many ways to the Grail tradition, which gave rise to Arthurian poems and made the myth famous. The transcending mystery that pours from the sacred vessel is a constant Iberian theme. It would be worth thorough investigation as it could throw up some surprising results.

Let us consider the fact that, for example, the traditional Grail celebration in the Christian world, which Wagner embodied in the culminating scenes of Parisfal, *was Good Friday. However, Spain (and not just the Spanish Church, but the entire population, in a strange symbiosis with ecclesiastical authority) instituted Corpus Christi as a fundamental celebration, with a view to favouring the mysterious sanctity of transubstantiation. At ecclesiastical levels, this feast stands out on account of its grandiloquent display of the numerous monstrances intended to house the sacred cup. This display takes the form of popular civic parades in Valencia as well as Toledo, Oñate, Seville, Berga, Zamora, Pollença, Barcelona, Medina de Rioseco, Cadiz, Daroca and Sitges. They bring the population together to pay a mass tribute to the chalice of the Passion with its holy and life-giving significance.*

In Spain, the most profound pagan versions of the Holy Grail myths are also told relatively frequently. An example, though tied to other Grail connections, occurred in Pola de Somiedo in the Asturian region. The venerated chalice was stolen from a nymph in the parish of Santiago de Aquino by a townswoman. She sneaked off with it while the mythical being was busy shining gold. In the village of Somiedo they say that the nymph then sang:

If you want it for Santiago
Why did you not ask for it?

It was in Najera… where the knightly order of the Terrace was founded, which was in essence of Holy Grail inspiration. And probably no less so was the fancy dress street party held in Monarrón, Alcarria. Among other activities, there was a feast in the presence of a holy receptacle they called 'the pretty jar'.

It is noteworthy that Spain was where adapted versions of the Holy Grail legend immediately appeared. It is also very like-

ly to be where, probably in the second half of the fourteenth century, The quest for the Holy Grail *appeared, after the first book* The Cry of Merlin the Wise *had been tremendously popular among Spanish readers. The first book inspired a multitude of Iberian chivalrous tales including Cervantes' Don Quixote. Some of the epic medieval poems from Castilla — Infantes de Lara in particular — contain traditions heavily influenced by the Grail, similar in many ways to those that appeared in the same period, such as the stories written by Chrétien de Troyes, Eschenbach or Robert de Boron. This poem and many others have come down to us by way of their Romanesque version. Together, they form a Grail literature, which was subject, at some points, to a strong influence from beyond the Pyrenees. This influence gave rise to a very specific chivalrous ideology, imbued with such mysticism that even Saint Teresa of Jesus would have been intrigued by its transcendental adventures.*

And the seeds were scattered

The religious aspect of the Grail tradition in Spain and throughout the world can be summarised using an expression similar to this one: 'it sows the seeds of the most beautiful traditions that will grow into trees impossible to fell'. This impossibility is due to the fact that the traditions became rooted in popular culture. The literature that emerged from it was extremely rich in symbolism.

Yet let us not ignore an evident fact in Grail literature. Chrétien de Troyes based his work on Celtic legends, or other as yet undiscovered writings. Other authors who followed him introduced modifications while blatantly plagiarising his work, though in those times intellectual robbery among writers was not considered to be an offence.

As for the Grail enigma, we leave it in your hands. The fact that so many countries, cities and towns claim to be home to the Grail or to have kept it in their temple makes us think that the task of identifying the real one is impossible. Furthermore, the Grail could have been the cup the Queen of Sheba gave to Solomon, the chalice at the Last Supper or any other holy vessel that is connected with the origins of a religion or the creation of a race.

In spite of everything, this myth is so wonderful that even if it were not true, mankind would need to invent it, as, although we only value it as a literary milestone, it is, in fact, a key element in universal culture.

A beautiful princess could also knight a future seeker of the Grail chimaera.

BIBLIOGRAPHY

Alpuente, Moncho: *El enigma del Santo Grial*
Alvar, Carlos: *Demanda del Santo Grial*
Atienza, Juan García: *La rebelión del Grial*
Atienza, Juan García: *El Santo Grial*
Atienza, Juan García: *Guía de la España griálica*
Blanche, Winder: *Stories of King Arthur*
Cirlot, María Victoria: *La novela artúrica*
Chrétien de Troyes: *Le conte du Graal*
Day, David and Lee, Alan: *Castles of Legend*
Eslava Galán, Juan: *Los templarios y otros enigmas medievales*
Evola, Julius: *Mystery of the Grail*
Godwin, Malcolm: *The Holy Grail*
Malory, Sir Thomas: *Le Morte D'Arthur*
Mañe, Pablo: *El rey Arturo y los caballeros de la Tabla Redonda*
Markale, Jean: *Le cycle du Graal*
Matthews, John: *Holy Grail*
Matthews, John: *Grail tradition*
Pastoureau, Michel: *La vie quotidienne en France et en Angleterre au temps des chevaliers de la Table Ronde*
Rahn, Otto: *El Grial y el milagro cátaro*
Resina, Joan Ramón: *La búsqueda del Grial*
Rique, Martín de: *Las leyendas del Grial y otros temas épicos medievales*
Usero, Rafael: *Sir Lanzarote do Lago e a sua proxenie cedeiresa*
Vázquez Alonso, Mariano: *La leyenda del Santo Grial*
Misterios de lo Desconocido: Búsquedas Míticas (Time-Life. Edition Prado)

INDEX

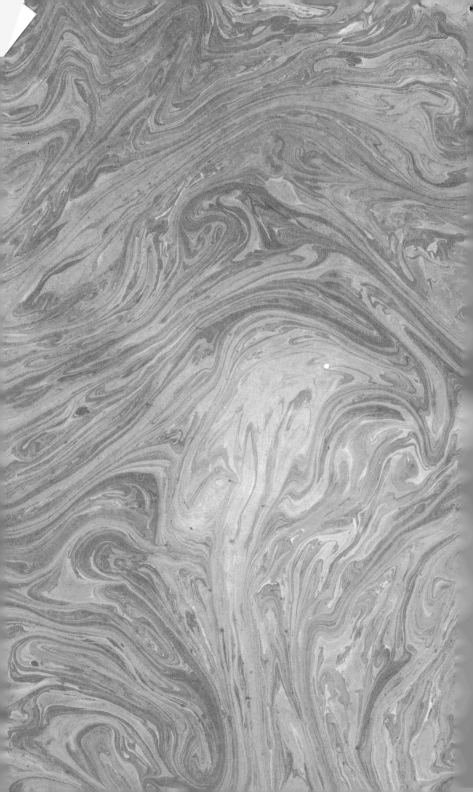